THE BASIC OFFICE ORGANISATION BOOK FOR START-UPS

DR ANSHUMALI PANDEY | SHAMBHU NATH GAUTAM

Copyright © Dr Anshumali Pandey, Shambhu Nath Gautam
All Rights Reserved.

Contents

Foreword

What is a paperless office?

A paperless office is a workplace that has minimal paper-based processes and relies on digitized documents instead. Some organizations prefer the term "paper-light" as many offices and departments cannot completely eliminate paper files because of process or compliance requirements.

Regardless, reducing the use of paper helps accelerate an organization's digital transformation journey. This typically involves transitioning to an electronic document managing system that digitizes files and stores it in a central repository.

The benefits of going paperless

Corporations in the US spend more than $120 billion per year on printed forms alone, most of which become obsolete within three months and end up in the trash. On top of that, office workers spend 30-40 percent of their time looking for documents in physical file cabinets.

Some of the most paper-intense departments are human resources, accounts payable and receivable, facilities management and customer service, which deal with a high volume of applications, resumes, receipts, work orders, invoices, bills, and more.

Evidently, working with paper documents creates problems that prevent an employee from being productive and an organization from saving costs. Adopting a paperless system can solve these challenges and achieve benefits like:

A. **Saving time spent on locating and retrieving physical files.** Digital documents can be easily organized and indexed, which makes finding the files you need much faster with search capabilities. As documents become more accessible, the time taken to retrieve files is significantly cut down so your team can be more productive and focus on other high-value tasks.

B. **Promoting collaboration among team members.** Staff are able to share files digitally without printing and view updated and past versions of documents. This minimizes the steps and optimizes the workflow when working together on documents.

C. **Improving security of information**. Access rights can be assigned and revoked according to user level and document type. With granular security settings, confidential and sensitive information can be tracked and protected against misuse and unauthorized changes. This also reduces the risk of loss and theft.

D. **Saving costs spent on printing and storing documents**. Eliminating the majority of paperwork helps you save money spent on paper and filing cabinets, as well as other costs like photocopier ink and office stationery.

How to transform into a paperless office

A document management system captures and stores information digitally on a single platform with integrated search options. In order to ease the change from paper to digital, you can start by:

a. **Determining the right solution**. The platform that you deploy should address and solve your unique business needs and challenges, with the flexibility to adapt to changes and scale with growth.

b. **Starting the digitizing process**. This is likely the most challenging part because of the time and labour involved. The magnitude of the work depends on how many paper files there are to begin with. However, with the help of your solutions provider, you can work on a strategy to tackle the digitizing process that can then be implemented as best practices for employees.

c. **Instilling change management**. A crucial part of any successful transformation initiative is gaining buy-in from stakeholders. Help your team understand the need for change and how a new system helps them become more productive, impactful and valuable in their work. Develop a training program to prepare employees on handling new processes and gather feedback from them for further improvement.

As with any change, it will take time for your organization to adjust. It is recommended to start on a smaller scale with critical processes that have the most impact from going paperless, before scaling the solution to other processes and departments.

Best Wishes,

Dr Anshumali Pandey, Author.

Preface

Office Organisation for Start-ups:

If you're a budding entrepreneur finding your way in the workforce, then you know how important it is to assemble the best team possible. And part of that equation means getting your start-up company to run with efficiency.

Whether you're one of the 69 percent of entrepreneurs who start their businesses from home, or operate in a noisy shared workspace, getting organized is a sure-fire recipe for success.

Something as simple as clearing off your desk can have a major positive effect on your productivity. In fact, researchers say all it takes is a pile of clutter to zap you of the energy you need to stay on task. Rather than spin your wheels on a daily basis, consider the value a boost in your productivity can provide.

Take a look at the five office organization tips below to help get your start-up one step closer to thriving.

With the freelance job market on the rise, there's no better time to crank up your start-up. In fact, with the start-up hiring rate climbing to a five-year high, 80 percent of entrepreneurs are planning to hire. That's why it's vital to try these five ideas to help get your office organized so you can focus more on success.

1. Go Green

No matter what type of office you have – home or commercial space – the amount of paper you have seems to breed on a daily basis. Instead of building the "leaning tower of paper," consider buying recycling bins to keep the piles at a minimum.

2. The Power of the Purge

Keeping your visual space clear can also help keep your mind clear to work on projects throughout the day. Take a day, or a week, to go through every single item you have in drawers, file cabinets, and on your desk, and ask yourself if it is helping – or hurting – your productivity. Donate unused items to a thrift store and recycle any paper or plastic materials for a clear conscience.

3. Digitize It All

If you're a start-up company, chances are you are clinging to a ton of papers, forms, and tax receipts for those "just in case I need it" moments. But we're here to tell you to get with the 21st Century and the digital world. Invest in a scanner and get to work scanning and storing all of your paperwork and important stuff on both a hard drive and in the cloud for easy access.

4. Bin There, Organized That

If you're already an organized person, you might already know the benefits of having organizational tools like bins and trays to tidy up your desk. But for the rest of us, knowing how to organize our desks with these items is the perfect gateway to productivity.

Start with two trays, one for incoming tasks and one for outgoing tasks, to keep things simple. Implement more as your projects develop but remember not to go overboard with stacks of trays – you still want to keep your desk manageable.

5. Drawers Are Your Secret Weapon

Give your desk a good clearing off and remove all of the knick-knacks, wacky magnets, and other nonsense that distracts you from being your best at work. Put all of your favourite items in a drawer to maximize space and minimize daily distractions.

Remember to put your most used files in the drawer next to your desk for easy access. Organizing your files with online labels is an excellent organizational tool to help you stay in the game.

So friends, once you've created a better office space, you'll reap the productivity rewards.

Shambhu Nath Gautam, Author

Prologue

Importance of Computer in Office Work:

The importance of computer in office enables the utilization of "productive" office software tools that facilitate effective management of data processing documentation, extensive numerical calculations and outputs that are useful in deciding, and quite complex but highly organized collections of varied sorts of data, which can be alphabetical, numerical, or both. Again the latter functions leave quick and straightforward management, of business data, that facilitate quick office operations thereby producing useful business information like billing and invoices. In this regard, office software tools, like the Microsoft Software Suite of productive tools, are a basic feature of just about every modern office computer software.

Modern computer networks facilitate business interactions among offices in small and enormous businesses and also promote productive two ways or multi-path business flows with other remote business, governmental, legal, and commercial, and almost the other relevant or related business concerns. Intrinsically they extend and augment the reach and capability of the office enterprise.

The office computer has therefore leaped forward from being a mere facilitator of platforms for data processing, spreadsheets, databases, and PowerPoint presentations to being a dynamic and interactive business instrument for offices in contemporary times.

Communication:

The importance of computer in office is the best communication process. Internal and external communications are much easier with the use of emails and internal messaging systems on computers. Office personnel are able to pass information through the office quickly and effectively, and most work environments have an alert system on individual computers when a new message or email is received. The Internet also improves communication options with Skype and other communication programs that allow national or international video conferences with ease and lower cost.

Data Storage:

The storage and removal of data from computers get better as technology advances. Files can be easily retrieved via search functions, and hard drives can store unprecedented volumes of files and data. For offices with large databases, such as government, charities, and other member-based associations, these storage features provide unprecedented advantages over traditional paper file storage, as well as the ease and speed of removal of the file, information, the ease of changing records, the ease of tracking changes made by a customer, member, or to find citizenship records.

Networking:

According to the Spam Laws website, file sharing is one of the key benefits of networked computers in an office. Office networks, or the creation of an office intranet, mean that a common database of files is accessible to all users. This also applies to software and computer management, which significantly reduces costs, as single network software can be purchased rather than buying multiple copies for each computer. Networks also provide common access to printers, fax machines, and copiers.

Productivity:

Computers in the office environment significantly improve productivity. According to the Reference for Business website, computers in the office increase productivity not only in areas such as word processing, data management, and access to information, but also in information creation, sharing, and ultimately storage. However, the amount of time most workers spend at a computer has increased myriad problems such as fatigue in the eyes, wrists, and hands.

CHAPTER ONE

MODERN OFFICE AND ITS FUNCTIONS

INTRODUCTION

Office is described as the nerve center of an organization. It has become an indispensable part of any business organization. Present-day office activities have expanded tremendously to keep pace with the rapid globalization. Modern offices organized on scientific principles with their techno-savvy office managers allow the sustenance of business amidst cut-throat competition.

In olden days, all jobs in the organization were mostly done by the proprietors. If work was more two or three more persons were appointed. They had to sit in small rooms and worked in a poorly lighted and congested place. There were no modern office amenities as of today; clerks were found copying letters tiresomely turning leather-bound registers. Typewriters had not come into general use, most of the office work had to be performed manually, and clerks would be found spending most of their time copying letters for dispatch to customers. All the internal and external communications were performed through human agency. The telephones and intercom systems were not generally in use. The proprietor of business would be found sitting in the office room and supervising the office work. He personally was responsible for dealing with customers and visitors. In the past, production was generally from a limited number of locally available raw materials, whereas marketing was in most cases confined to local markets. Businessmen were interested in maximizing profits through two important profit centres, i.e. production and marketing. A few decades ago, the office was defined as a place for clerical work within the four walls of a building.

Office activities have undergone profound changes in the last few decades. The world has witnessed spectacular advancements in the field of science, technology, industrialization, transport, communication, etc. In modern terms, office is viewed as a function. When it is taken as a function, it (Office) may direct, control and coordinate the office work wherever it is done and whosoever does it. Here it may be noted that in modern times, offices are developed on scientific principles, and their management and administration is in the hands of qualified and trained managerial staff.

THE OFFICE AND OFFICE WORK:

Meaning of Office-

Office is a place for transacting business where clerical and administrative functions are carried out to coordinate and control activities of an organization. A typical office performs tasks such as framing business policies, processing and communication of information, record keeping, and handling e-mails, execution of orders, managing receipts, and payments. An office can be described as any place where information converges on paper, is documented, preserved and used for both current and future operation of businesses.

In the past few decades, office activities have undergone vast changes. The old dingy, cluttered, stuffy office rooms have vanished have been replaced by well-ventilated, well-lit, air-conditioned offices with up to date furnishings in alluring designs. Gone are the days when the head of the concern had to personally supervise the work of clerks. Today, modern offices are organized on scientific principles and their management and administration are in the hands of a specialized office manager. Managers do not share the same room with clerks but sit in separate rooms. The clerks are supervised and controlled with the help of supervisors and through standard office systems, routines, office manuals, etc.

Advancements, in the recent past, have led to an expansion in the scale of production and business activities as the size of business enterprises grows; there is a corresponding increase in the volume of office work.

The office activities of today are not performed by general clerks but by specialized clerks – Receptionist, Cashier, Typist, Telephone Operators, etc. There is also a higher division of labour. Departmentalization of office has been affected. The office managers of today welcome greater use of machines and minimal use of human beings in the office work. Machines-typewriter, telephones, computers, calculators, duplicating machines, Dictaphones, accounting machines, intercom, cellular phones, internet system, etc help save time and labour. Computers are the latest additions to the long list of office machines, capable of performing most clerical operations at high speed without errors. Thus, modern offices are embracive to more and more technical advancements.

Office is an important section of business. The term business implies office work. The office is defined as "a place for the transaction of business, the room or department, where the clerical work is done," or we can say "a place where business is carried on", or it is "a place where all sorts of activities of organization are dealt with". An office is the centre of an organization. Commercial office acts as a central directing and coordinating agency of the various activities of any business.

In the modern age, the "office" is used in a broader sense. An office is to a business what the mainspring is to a watch. An organization cannot be carried on without an office, as a watch without the mainspring is useless. In present times, the modern office organization has so much importance as the brain in a human body. Thus, a commercial office can be called "a clearing house of all essential business information". The office has to receive or collect all information of the business, process the collected information (analyses, arrange and classify) and put them into an understandable form on the one hand. On the other hand, the processed information has to be presented or communicated to the management of the business as and when required.

According to the Random House Dictionary "An office is a place where business is transacted or professional services are available" An office is the place where the control mechanisms for an enterprise are located, records are initiated for communication, control and efficient operation of the enterprise. According to Mills and Standing Ford, "The office is the administrative centre of a business". The purpose of an office has been defined as the providing of a service of communication and record.

It is generally seen, in commercial offices, there are some persons to receive information, process them and supply the processed information to the management. Doing so can be called a clerical job. Clerical job includes correspondence (to collect information or clarify the information received) serving (filing), typing, book-keeping, handling of money, etc.

Efficient management of the organization helps the managers or executives to formulate planning, organizing, controlling, and supervise activities. Prompt and accurate decision depends upon timely information.

An office is a place to record the information for control through collection (of information) handled and serviced. The control mechanism for a business is located-paper work is to attain an aimed result. One must give importance to the office function rather than to the place. An office is a place of paper processing and memory centre for all its departments. In the office, policies and ideas are formulated through collection and analysis of obtained information. An office maintains all records. And this readymade, scrutinized and processed information is made available to the management to attain the best result.

Office Work-

According to the old concept "Office work" is mostly concerned with clerical work where the records of an enterprise and making, preserving the records for further usage. Office work not only deals with records, it also includes communication, mechanical data processing, planning and scheduling.

Office work being mainly concerned with clerical work or paper work is narrow view and an old concept of office work. Nowadays, office work has a very wide scope. Office work is primarily concerned with making, preserving, and using records. The records are concerned about purchasing, producing, selling, accounting and correspondence, inventories, and written or printed memorandum of all kinds. These records are essential for an efficient and effective control of the organization.

An office serves as the memory centre and control organ of an organization. The office performs many services like communication, reproduction, mechanical data, processing, procuring of stationery, furniture and equipment, secretarial assistance, etc to other departments in an organization.

Office is a unit where relevant records for control, planning and efficient management of the organization are prepared, handled and preserved. Office provides facilities for internal and external communication as well as coordinates activities of different departments of the organization. The purposes of an office are:

- To preserve all the records of the business.
- To handle incoming correspondence.
- To plan the policies of the business and ensure their implementation.
- To direct and co-ordinate the activities of the various department.

- To maintain accounts, statutory and non-statutory books, etc of the business.

Office Activities-

Each office has a personality of its own. This personality is a reflection of the purpose of the existence of an office. The manufacturing office has a profile that differs from that of the sales office. Likewise, the accounting office has a different orientation from that of a research and development office. In organizing a new office, the office manager must first determine the prime reason for the existence of that office and then add the necessary ingredients to bring about an efficient operation entity that achieves predetermined results.

Although offices differ from one another in prime responsibility, many activities are commonly carried out by all the offices. Some of these activities are:

- Processing incoming mail.
- Processing outgoing mail.
- Maintenance of the records (Filing and Indexing).
- Establishing standard at office work.
- Designing and procuring at office forms, stationery, etc.
- Recruitment and training of office staff.
- Maintenance of furniture, machines, appliances, etc.
- Preparation of statements, reports, etc.
- Maintenance of accounts and other financial records.
- Handling Telephone calls and enquiries.
- Preparing updated information for the whole firm.

- Arranging the data in a quick and accessible form for using and safeguarding the assets.
- Keeping prompt and accurate handling of enquiries orders etc.
- Maintaining an efficient flow of work in the office.

IMPORTANCE OF AN OFFICE:

Purpose of an office-

The place of office is incomparable as it fulfills the following purposes:

- It is a place where the management can prepare the plans intelligently.
- The management can make their plans effective from the office.
- From the office, records of the progress of plan in action can be obtained.
- Through different control techniques carried out in the office with available records, the effectiveness of the plan in action can be ascertained.
- The results of such action are evaluated in the office without delay.
- Different activities are coordinated from the office.

Importance of an Office-

"No organization worth its name can exist without an office". Thus, the office is an essential segment of any organization, big or small, govt. or private and contributes to its efficient and economical functioning. The importance of an office to a business organization is high because of the variety and complications that a business enterprise faces due to competition, legal and statutory restrictions, role of trade unions and a host of other factors. A business enterprise today cannot stand without the assistance of a well-organized office.

Office is behind every business activity and the nerve centre of all deliberations. In the words of Dicksee, what office is to business is what the man spring is to watch. All operations are directed, coordinated and controlled through the office. A well-organized office makes it possible for management to plan its operations intelligently, appraise results and coordinate all the activities of the business.

The term office has been defined in a variety of ways. In general terms, office means a place where clerical work is performed and all kinds of paperwork is maintained & dealt. However, in modern sense of the term, office denotes an activity and not a place. Whenever clerical operations are performed, they are treated as office function. According to Edward Roche "It is a mistake to regard the office as a specific place; instead an office exists anywhere, wherever certain kinds of works are performed".

Office is regarded as an important part of an organization. The very existence of an organization necessitates the presence of an office whether a government institution, business house or an educational institution. Office plays a pivotal role in its functioning because a well-managed office helps management to plan its operation intelligently and to put them in action competently. Without an efficient office, business activities cannot be carried on systematically. The importance of an office can be defined in the following ways:

a. **Information Center:** Office is an information center or a data bank of all information on which the business is carried. All present and past figures of business that it does should be in the office. Based on this information, the office plans, and forecasts and controls its operation and its area of operation.

b. **Channel of Communication**: It is evident that without any communication, the office cannot all alone function and serve its purpose. Every communication, especially the written communication flows from the top to the bottom, and the reporting has to flow from the bottom to the top. The office would fall if the flow of communications is not frequent and the reports are not made available or presented to the higher authorities within the stipulated time.

c. **Aids in Coordination**: The objectives of any office won't be met if there is no proper coordination among the employees. The employer-employee relation and the employee-employee relation have to be strong if effective coordination has to be built up. An effective coordination jacks up the spirit of work tightens the unity and strengthens the morale of every employee working in the organization. Moreover, the necessary information and feedback from the top level is needed for promoting coordination.

d. **Importance in Relation to Government and Public:** Today, for every business to exist, it has to follow certain guidelines, rules and regulations as formulated by the government. Every business unit today is considered to be revenue-generating as well as a social institute. Every office has a wing, and it is a link between society and the government. It is also a link between the people and the government. Hence, an office has to create a proper type of image in the mind of the people for building a proper brand image and a corporate image.

e. **Aid in Managerial Control:** Control is a combination of corrective and measuring techniques of the performance of subordinates in order to make sure that the objective of an enterprise is achieved and accomplished. Control requires establishing 'standards' and then measuring the standards within the stipulated time and resources.

f. **Importance in Relation to Customers:** The actual importance of any office is its relation with its customer. It is the customer who brings the business to the office and, hence, a customer is the king. Except for the government office, every other business organization depends on its customer for its business to generate the revenue. Hence, the importance of office about its customer is of great significance "customer", now, is the 'emperor'. The orders received by the customer, their enquiries and their complaints are taken care by the office through direct and personal contacts. Nowadays, the modern office has a very important person—the Guest Attending Officer who attends all the customers and informs them everything directly, personally, or on the phone, about the company, its activities, and about its business.

g. **Importance to Shareholder:** Every office serves an important link between the shareholder on the one hand and the company on the other. The issue of division of shares, transfer of the shares, issue of the notice of the meetings of the company, and answering about all the queries to the shareholder is of great importance and these cannot be achieved or obtained without establishing a proper office.

h. **Importance of the Worker:** For maintaining a good workforce, a good environment, free from official politics, free from partiality and an effective relation, in the form of employee-employer and employer-employee a relationship is needed.

FUNCTIONS OF THE OFFICE

An office is primarily concerned with the collection and supply of information. Accurate and up-to-date information relating to the organization and other agencies affecting the organization is always required for taking decisions and formulating policies. Besides, office has assumed many other responsibilities, such as safeguarding assets, personnel management, and procurement of assets, etc. which are incidental to the primary function. Therefore, the functions of a modern office may be classified into two categories: [i] Basic functions [ii] Administrative functions.

Basic Functions

Basic functions are those functions of an office which need to be performed in all types of organizations. They are mainly related to receiving and giving of information. These basic functions are as follows:

- **Collecting Information:** The office receives or collects information about various activities of the organization. The information may be collected from internal or external sources. Internal sources may be employees and various departments of the organization. The external sources are customers, suppliers and government departments, etc. From internal sources, information may be received in the form of letters, circulars, reports, etc. and external sources provide information through letters, orders, invoices, inquiries, reports, questionnaires, etc. The executives of the organization may also collect information while visiting other organizations.

- **Recording Information:** The office keeps a record of information collected from various sources to make it readily available to the management. The information is kept in the form of correspondence, reports, statements, circulars, lists, charts, registers, books, etc. An office has to also maintain records as prescribed under law. The registered office of a company is required to maintain Register of Members under the Companies Act, 1956.

- **Arranging, Analyzing and Processing the Information:** The information collected in an office is generally not in the form to be used by the management. Therefore, facts and figures collected have to be arranged, processed, organized and analyzed to make them useful to the management. In this regard, financial statements, statistical statements, charts, lists, reports and summaries are prepared.

- **Preserving Information:** The information is properly sorted out and preserved in the most economic and scientific manner. Various types of equipment, filing cabinets, etc. are used for preserving records. Unnecessary and outdated records are destroyed to make space for new and valuable records.

- **Supplying information:** All accumulated and processed information is useless unless it is communicated. The office serves as a two-way channel for communication. On the one hand, it supplies the collected, recorded and processed information to the management. On the other hand, the policy decisions, guidelines and instructions issued by the management to the departments are also routed through the office. The information may be supplied verbally or in writing.

Administrative Functions-

Administrative functions are in addition to the basic functions. Nevertheless, the office cannot hope to work smoothly without them. These relate to the tasks of protecting and safeguarding assets, maintaining and enhancing the operating efficiency, stationery control, choice and use of the office equipment's and selection, training, placement, and remuneration of the personnel. The following functions are normally considered as administrative functions of an office:

- **Management Functions:** Various functions of management are also applicable to the management of office functions. Office work has to be planned, organized and executed according to the plan. Control is exercised to ensure the efficiency of operations in the office. Staffing, directing, communicating, co-ordination and motivating is also important for the management of offices.
- **Instituting Office Systems and Routines:** An office has to develop systems and procedures for providing better services to other departments. Each phase of office work is carefully analyzed, and a proper procedure is developed for it. Proper sequencing of different tasks is necessary to ensure the continuous flow of work.
- **Procuring Stationery and Supplies:** Adequate supply of quality office stationery is necessary for the efficient performance of office work. The

office purchases standard quality paper, pens, ink and other stationery items, maintain the stock and issue them only on demand.

- **Designing and Control of Office Forms:** Use of standardized forms simplifies office operations. It is the responsibility of the office to design, standardize, provide and control the forms to be used in the office and other departments of the enterprise.
- **Purchasing Office Equipment and Furniture:** Efficient and economical performance of office work requires proper furniture, equipment and machines. The office has to arrange for the selection and purchase of these items from reliable suppliers. It also has to ensure timely availability of furniture, etc. to departments and employees and facilitate proper utilization, as well as arrange for maintenance, servicing and replacement according to needs.
- **Safeguarding Assets:** Different types of assets are maintained in an organization. The assets must be protected against damages and losses on account of fire, theft, etc. An efficient control system is exercised by the office to safeguard the assets.
- **Personnel Management:** The efficiency of office work depends very much on the employees. Their appointment, training, promotion, appraisal and welfare are the functions of the office.
- **Maintaining Public Relations:** An organization depends on public reputation and goodwill for its existence and progress. Maintaining public relations is also the responsibility of the office. Most organizations have reception counters to greet and receive visitors to the organization.

THE CHANGING OFFICE

Office Yesterday

A few decades ago, a typical business Office presented a gloomy picture. Housed in one or two small rooms, poorly lighted and ill-ventilated, it was generally situated in the least conspicuous part of the building. There was a small volume of paperwork, which was handled by a few clerks manually and without the aid of mechanical and labour-saving devices. Since typewriters were somewhat rare, the clerks had to do all the written work with their own hands. Letters were copied before dispatch on loose sheets or in fat leather-bound registers. All the internal and external communication was performed or carried on through the human agency, for telephones and intercom systems were not generally in use. The proprietor of a business or the head clerk would be found sitting in the office room, supervising and guiding office work, and personally dealing with the visitors or customers. There was no departmentalization of office activities, and the techniques of scientific management were either not known or not practiced.

Historical Developments.

The following technological developments made during the last 150 years have led to the evolution of the modern office:

1870: First commercial typewriter introduced. 1880: Alexander Graham Bell invented telephone. 1920: Electric typewriter introduced.

1930: Important machines like duplicators, Dictaphones, intercoms developed.

1950: Calculators, computers, copying machines, addressographs, and franking, tabulating and accounting machines developed.

1961: Memory electronic typewriters launched.

1964: Word processing equipment, cash registers, etc.

1970: Introduction of digital networks local area networks (LAN). 1980: Computerized telephone networks, picture phone, etc.

1990: Personal computers, micro processing equipment, electronic mail, fax machines, modems, pagers, Cellular Phones, Internet Systems, etc.

2000: Internet Banking, Internet Trading, BPO servicing, Internet Telephony, Digitized office.

2008: Apple I-Phones, Voice Mails, Teleconferencing, Handwriting and speech Recognition Software, Broadband Spectrum, L.C.D. and Plasma T.V.s. 3D image Videoconferencing (telepresence), etc., Black Berry, Google Gphone, Robotics, etc.

2012: Voice/Face/Handwriting Recognition, 3D Printing, Apple iPhones 4S, ITB Hard Disk,

2014: Blue Ray Disc, Voice Navigation, Wi-fi, Wireless Printers, Cloud Computing (Google Drive, DropBox, Skydrive-Microsoft), iPad, Business Analytics (for Cash Management, Website Management, Employee Management, etc.) SaaS (Software as a Service), LED, Mobile Banking, Virtualization, Android, Ubuntu, Internet of Things (IOT), etc.

Office Today

Office activities have undergone vast changes in the last five-six decades. A modern office is well-planned, well-laid out and well-organized. The scope of office activities has widened tremendously following spectacular developments in science and technology, industrialization, transport and communication. These developments have led to an expansion in the scale of production and business activities, to greater governmental and legislative interference and control, and the consequent enlargement of the volume of office work. In today's office, activities are performed not by general-purpose clerks but by specialized clerks- by receptionists, accounts clerks, cashiers, stenographers and typists. There is, thus, a greater division of labour. Loose-leaf binders have replaced the old fat leather-bound ledgers. Filing and indexing techniques have been developed. Departmentalization of office has been affected. Greater and wider use of machines (typewriters, dictaphones, calculators, accounting machines, computers, etc.) is made to save time and labour. Work standardization, job evaluation, merit rating and other techniques of personnel management are being practiced. Telephones, intercoms, telex and other communication device, are used for rapid and global communication. Many large-sized offices use computers to handle the enormous volume of work. The use of carbonless copy paper has become very popular.

In short, Offices today are organized on scientific principles, and their management and

administration are in the hands of highly specialized managers. The term "Office Management" is rapidly being replaced by the term "Administrative Office Management" and "Information Management"

Office of the Future

Advancements in technology are having an enormous impact on the working of the office. The new office technologies are converting the information that was written or typed, transmitted and stored on paper to be processed by computer-based machines more accurately and at much higher speed. However, it may be stressed that the rate of introduction of the new technology is very 'variable' and it might take many years before all offices resemble 'office of the future'. In India, we usually find a mixture of traditional and new machines in the same office. Few organizations have the finance or are prepared to take the risk of replacing all their old office equipment with the new machines all at once. We are, in fact, in a period of transition which might extend to a few years or even more. In the more distant future, we might see an office that is virtually 'paperless'. However, in the near future, there will be an important reduction rather than a total abolition of paperwork.

The office of the future has to face a variety of challenges — social, political and economic. For instance, with the increased mechanization of office activities and the installation of sophisticated machines like computers, it seems we are on the threshold of office automation. With the increasing pace of industrialization and government control of the business, the need to employ more experts and specialists to perform office activities has become pressing, and has led to the utilization of consultancy services to a greater extent. These developments call for a greater "professionalization of management" and increased application of the principles of management to the office. The other challenges faced by the office of the future include:

- The challenge of legal provisions.
- The challenge of reducing paperwork.
- The challenge of reducing office cost.

Once these challenges are met, the productivity of an office would increase, and its importance would be enhanced in relation to the business organization of the future.

THE PAPERLESS OFFICE

The 21st-century offices will be an electronic wonderland where expensive paper-based routine work will be replaced by result-oriented and advanced information technology. Office automation, with its micro-circuitry and visual display screens, is sure to take over the old and worn-out methodology, in office management. Probably, within the next 3-5 years, office information system would be installed and developed to such an extent that it would replace the desk, the typewriter, the filing cabinet and the plethora of paperwork.

With the evolution of a new work style, based on speed, accuracy and efficiency the offices which fail to wake up to the implications of modern information technology will find themselves lagging behind. They would become vulnerable to the technological onslaught of their better-equipped competitors. A US study16 on office automation has indicated that 100% of the banking industry has already installed Office automation systems of some kind. An average of 85-word processors per 1,000 employees was reported. Together with these, the banks are likely to add private videotext, electronic mail, online management information systems with graphics and voice information systems. Future developments also imply the adoption of multifunctional workstations with a wide variety of capabilities. The technological advances have also invaded offices in Europe, UK, Japan, etc. However, in India, the position has started to emerge, and in certain sectors, rapid computerization is taking place particularly in BPOs, Stock Market Operations, Banking, Retailing, Higher Education, etc. The concept of paperless office encompasses the following:

- The omnipresent desk will now be replaced by the multifunctional workstation with a personal computer linked to other personal computers via a high-speed Local Area Network (LAN) system. The workstation can be further linked to the main station so that the staff positioned at the workstations can contact and manipulate information from the Office records.
- Computers, equipped to process words as well as figures, will replace typewriters. The present-day, word processor will slowly give way to personal computers.
- The electronic-magnetic or optical-filing is the one to succeed the paper filled filing cabinets in our offices. Microfilming will also reduce paper records and facilitate the retrieval of records.
- For outward communication, facsimile (FAX) system will replace the dispatch section.
- For inward communication, shorthand notebooks and typewriters will give way to dictating machines and printer computers.
- Desktop Publishing System will look after the entire printing work of the office. It will write and format documents, create and incorporate

graphics, prepare camera-ready copy for printing, keep databases of mailing and subscription lists, create official advertising files and brochures and keep all financial records, no matter how large or small it is.

- Various machines like accounting machines, billing machines, payroll machines, addressing and mailing machines, punched card machines, etc. shall be replaced by computer network (LAN) system.

- The automatic answering devices and automatic electronic branch exchanges will reduce the workload of the reception counter of the office.

- The new emphasis will be on LAN system- a low-cost method of connecting microcomputers, printers and data storage devices on a single site. Imaginative use of information technology helps to create new opportunities. It cuts down operating costs, provides faster and more accessible information and reduces time spent on clerical functions and unproductive tasks.

Are the days of paper limited?

The increasing use of office machines in transmission, storage and data processing has facilitated the offices to abandon the use of paper to a large extent. However, the realization of the goal of 'Paperless Office' is subjected to the following problems:

1. Transmission: Facsimile transmission is already possible, but it requires both the receiver and sender have compatible electronic apparatus, which will restrict transmission for some time to come.

2. Storing: Microfilm has long been used as a storage medium, but as yet it has made no serious in roads into the use of paper. Data storage of huge quantities of information is already carried out by computers. Nevertheless, the most used device of many computers is not video display units (VDU) but printer.

3. Data Processing: Again, computers already perform many data processing tasks which previously were being carried out by clerks armed only with pencils and paper. However, aspects like, financial, organizational and resistance to change will inhibit the rapid elimination of paper.

As such, the transformation of the office is not an easy task. An integrated approach where information is treated as a primary resource is necessary to reap maximum benefits from office automation. Further, the software supporting an electronic office should be reliable, accessible to everybody and easy enough to be operated by everybody irrespective of their ability or status, "Office automation can be carried out in a phased manner starting with the clerical staff and later moving on to the professionals and managers". Managers can have desktop on workstations, which can be used for electronic mail, finding information from large central databases and typing text while producing reports. Through a properly linked network system, a manager can send electronic messages to his colleagues and arrange meetings and appointments. He can also type letters from his own laptops (screen- based/workstation). For maximum results, the technology used should be matched to the needs of the business and business objectives. The person coordinating the 'Information Technology' (IT) activity must be familiar with the business objectives of the organization.

Tips for a Paperless Office

Many people who use computers- whether it's for their home or business- are moving towards a "paperless office". Simply, they are tired and overwhelmed by scraps of paper, heaps of old file folders, envelopes- and they want to reduce the clutter. Take a look at how many messages are stored in your e-mail's in-basket. Now imagine how much paper would have been generated if they hadn't come to you from cyberspace.

Many companies have made at least a partial move to a paperless office. They're doing so this way: by using scanners instead of copying machines, sending electronic faxes instead of paper faxes, storing information electronically instead of in filing cabinets, giving staff clients or vendor's information on CDs or through Internet attachments instead of inbound folders. In short, they're getting a greater return on their hardware, software and technology investments. Here are six things to keep in mind as you move towards a paperless home or business office.

a. **Without paper, make sure you're backing up files**. In the traditional backup system, you would make a photocopy of a document and put it in a properly-labeled folder that can later be retrieved from a filing cabinet. Many people and businesses develop electronic filing systems that mimic the old paper systems, using Microsoft Word or customized programs for storing documents by type of document, client, project or other prioritization. But those files can't just be created — they have to be backed up as well. Backup solutions can include backing up to second hard drives, to removable drives or to Internet and off-site locations to minimize the risk of loss of data from a computer failure. So, the message here is to have a system in place for regular and consistent backing up of your information.

b. **Realize that a paperless office doesn't happen overnight**. Your home office or business won't go from all-paper one day-to-paperless the next. It's a progression. You might start out by scanning all incoming bills into your system and then expand to include all general business correspondence. Initially, you might imagine you're creating more work instead of less —especially if you run a business. It's just another way of backing up information.

c. **You'll need to rearrange your office** — a good thing. There usually aren't tremendous savings of office space when you first start focusing on using less paper. After all, you still have all those paper documents housed in your big, clunky file cabinets. At some point, during your transition to a 'paperless office', however, the difference in your physical storage space will become apparent.

d. **"Paperless" often really means "less paper"**. Yes. It's possible to scan all received documents into your computer and to store all in-house documents in your system as well. You can virtually eliminate paper faxes by generating faxes on your computer and having inbound faxes delivered to your computer system. You can even electronically sign or signature-stamp outgoing documents. But you're still likely to have some paper floating through your office. Not all of your clients or customers will want to be billed electronically. Some vendors will still want to communicate by snail mail. And tax and regulatory requirements could force you to either do some current business on paper or to keep hard copies of your past home or business records.

e. **Everyone has to participate in change**. Merely saying as head of household, owner or manager of a business that you want those around you to embrace your paperless office doesn't make it so. Your partner or staff has to buy into the transition as a permanently-new way of doing business. Change can be difficult. People who have been making photocopies, sending paper faxes, putting documents into legal-sized folders or saving tons of mail and catalogues that they just can't part with are going to have to change their perceptions. They will have to learn new routines that they already feel skilled at.

f. **Realize that less paper is just the beginning of the pay-off**. The most visible impact of a move to a paperless office is the reduction in the cost of printing, mailing, shipping and storing paper. Over time, lots of other benefits should become apparent: Less time spent looking for paper lost in the shuffle. Fewer hours looking for bills, documents and, if you're in business, copies of client documents. The ability to access all sorts of information from computer files, in a matter of seconds without having to search your office. If you've got a home office that serves as a satellite office of a business, you can have access to all of your business files, using a product like Terminal Services or other software, even if you're not at your business location. In short, change can be hard but it can be profitable.

Working towards the Paperless Office

The paperless office — promised since the first desktop computers started appearing in the 1980s- has yet to become a reality for most companies. Despite, the increasing use of computers in all types of businesses, a good portion of most day-to-day work is still paper- based. Besides, basic human behavior works against a truly 'paperless office', employees will always want to print documents for more careful study or to bring to meetings. For now, the perfect paperless office system remains an elusive goal.

Despite these challenges, you can drastically reduce the amount of paper documents your business depends on by choosing a document management system. The term "document management" (DM) covers a range of systems for managing paper and electronic files. To work towards a 'paperless office', a more specific term is "document imaging systems" which include tools to help convert paper records into electronic files.

Benefits of a Paperless Office Solution

It provides additional cost savings by eliminating paper records. Converting records rooms into usable office space can let you make much better use of expensive real estate, and to eliminate warehousing costs entirely. Other benefits include increased security, better disaster recovery protection, environmental benefits and remote access for your important documents.

The Automated Office

Till now, it was customary to transfer and store information on paper. With new electronic procedures and systems becoming more and more popular in use in modern automated office, the so-called "Paperless Office" is becoming a near reality. A 'Paperless Office' is one in which paper has been replaced by electronic, digital, micrographic and micro-processing systems and equipments. It is aptly said that. "The office is now in a period of transition" where more and more information processing functions are being automated through sophisticated electronic systems; the Paperless Office is attainable today."

"It may be noted that though paperwork can be reduced by up to 95 per cent in the traditional office, many people believe that a completely paperless office will not be attained in the near future."According to William Benedon in the 'Paperless Society; fact or fiction,' there are six major barriers to a totally paperless office; namely-

- Traditional Values.
- Legal Requirements.
- Accounting and Audit Values.
- Legislative Values.
- Societal Values and.
- Procedural Values.

In contrast, the System Analysts, Records Managers, and other management professionals often complain of the high cost of creating, storing, and retrieving, reproducing and disseminating paper documents.

Modern offices are increasingly converting all incoming and original data to either electronic form or microfilm, which can then be edited, indexed, stored, retrieved or converted to paper. In some companies' 'Paperless Office' integrates voice inputs, word processing, optical character recognition, electronic mail, calendars, message sending, filing directions and text editing, computer indexing and processing, COM, Micrographics, automated storage and retrieval, telecommunications and color graphics systems into a fully automated office facility.21 The integrated office has evolved into "Communicating Integrated Office". Office systems communicate with each other by the use of satellites. Several modern offices provide satellite communication, video teleconferences, and electronic mail and computer-to- computer hookups for intra-company use.

Subsystems of an Automated Office

The Modern Office System is said to have the following subsystems that are integrated into the Automated Office.

- Voice System.
- Word Processing.
- Optical Character Recognition (OCR).
- Data Processing.
- Reprographics.
- Micrographics
- Communication and Facsimile
- Graphic systems.
- Telecommunication (e.g. Teleconferencing, Videoconferencing, Computer conferencing, Telepresence [Latest innovation by CISCO Inc.])
- Electronic Mail.
- Photocomposition.
- Computer Networking
- Robotics

The business office is currently undergoing a dramatic change, an abrupt transition from antiquated procedures that have been evolved fundamentally for over a century to sophisticated, integrated systems involving electronic and advanced microcomputer technology.

The Virtual Office

A virtual office is an integrated suite of applications that is accessed via the internet and available 24/7. The 18 applications include calendar, address book, webmail, etc., and can also synchronize with PDA or Phone. One can receive agenda by SMS/Text Message every day and send SMS/Text message right out of virtual office. One may access the virtual office even from a pocket PC or mobile phone.

A virtual office may be created by an individual or maybe opened up to a group of employees, colleagues, vendors or anyone else within or outside the business. One can decide as to who joins, what to share and who can share what. Anyone who has access to the Internet has access to the virtual office, if allowed. The virtual office offers the following features:

- **Calendar:** Personal and group calendar. Share public events within your group, view another member's calendar and sync it with your PDA or wireless phone.
- **Address book:** Personal and group address book. Share public addresses within your group and view other member's addresses.
- **Web Mail:** Compose, send, receive, reply, forward e-mail with your new "@office.com" e-mail address. Includes POP3, folders, attachment, address books, templates, signature, anti-virus and anti-spam.
- **Documents:** Full document management centre with automatic backup. Share and jointly edit your personal or group's valuable information.
- **To Do's:** Be better organized. Manage your tasks, send tasks to other group members and control completion.
- **Forum:** Broadcast company news and ideas with your group effortlessly. Great for keeping everyone on the same page or brainstorming.
- **SMS:** Get your daily calendar by wireless phone via SMS (Short Message Service, commonly known as Text Messaging) or send reminders by SMS, send SMS directly from your address book.
- **Virtual Drive:** Using the virtual drive, you can access all your private and group documents directly from your PC or Mac computer.
- **Groups:** Create groups (or Virtual Offices) to share information with other members, such as addresses, documents, and bookmarks.

- **Meetings:** Schedule your meetings online in seconds and automatically invite others in your group to attend. See the responses as they roll in.
- **Calls:** Don't miss another important phone call. View a list of the calls "while you were absent," marking them off as you return to them.
- **Notes:** Create, save and stick notes to any object in your Organizer. Better than all those "Post-It" notes stuck to your monitor. Keeps the notes where you will see them, when you need them.
- **Reminders:** Meetings, birthdays, reminders on time of any events. Reminder displayed by screen pop up, e-mail, messages or SMS.
- **Bookmarks:** Save bookmarks which can be used from any browser, share them with other members.
- **Fax:** Using your messaging account, you can send faxes worldwide. You simply send a message in the same way that you send an e-mail.
- **Synchronize:** Synchronize your personal calendar, address book, tasks and notes with your PDA or PC. Whether it is Palm, Outlook, Lotus Organizer, iPAQ Pocket PC or

  Treo, you can sync up and run.

- **WAP:** Access your virtual office through WAP in order to check and enter information, using your WAP enabled wireless phone.
- **Encryption:** Use secured transfer when required (documents, calendars, addresses, or e-mails) or faster, non-secured transfer for no secure transfer.

POINTS TO REMEMBER:

- An office is generally understood to be a place where clerical work is performed and where all kinds of paperwork are done.
- Office activities include processing incoming mail, processing outgoing mail, Dictation, Transcription, Typing, Printing, Copying, Filing Records retrieval, Records disposal and Communication.
- The functions of a modern office may be classified into two categories: Basic Office Functions and Administrative Management Functions.
- Basic office functions include receiving information, recording information, arranging information and giving information.

- Administrative Office Functions include Management functions of planning, organizing, staffing, directing, communicating, controlling, coordinating and motivating, public relations function, instituting office systems and routines, retention of records, safeguarding assets, form designing and control, stationery and supplies control, selection and purchase of office appliances, personnel functions and controlling office costs.

- An office is an important and indispensable part of every organization, big or small. The importance of the office to a business enterprise arises from the fact that a modern business cannot be managed efficiently without clerical assistance in some form or other. The office serves modern business as an information centre, as an intermediary, as a coordinator, as a service centre, as an administrative nerve centre, as a control centre. It is rightly said that "the office is to a business what the main spring is to a watch".

- A paperless office is a concept in which usage of paper is greatly reduced or eliminated totally in an office environment. This is achieved by converting a document into digital form. According to the proponents, a paperless office is not only environmentally friendly, but also helps in boosting the productivity and efficiency of an office while also saving money and making work processes easier and more convenient as digital documents can be easily shared between users.

GLOSSARY:

- Office: It is the nerve centre of the entire organization.
- Administrative: Relating to or responsible for administration.
- Management: The art of getting things done.
- Front office: It welcomes visitors.
- Middle Office: It is usually a part of the operations division.
- Electronic office or e-office: Computer based office.
- Virtual office: Being actual or in almost every respect.
- Back office: Building layout of early organization where tasks dedicated to the operating company.
- Organization: It means a group of people who are cooperating under the direction of leadership for the accomplishment of communed.

- Automated: The technique of operating a process by electronic devices, reducing human intervention
- Paperless Office: Operating an office with minimum use of paper
- Filing: Keeping papers in order.
- Computing: To calculate or estimate.
- Execution: Performing or Accomplishing.
- Documented: Collection and keeping documents in order to be done
- Maintenance: Act of protection.
- Communication: Process of passing information.

CHAPTER TWO

OFFICE MANAGEMENT

INTRODUCTION

Management is a vital aspect of the economic life of man, which is an organized group activity. A central directing and controlling agency is indispensable for a business concern. Resources like material, labour, capital, etc. are entrusted to the organizing skill, administrative ability and enterprising initiative of the management. Thus, management provides leadership to a business enterprise without able managers and effective managerial leadership; the resources of production remain merely resources and never a final product. Under competitive economy and ever-changing environment, the quality and performance of managers determine both the survival as well as the success of any business enterprise. Management occupies such an important place in the modern world that the welfare of the people and the destiny of the country are very much influenced by it.

NATURE OF MANAGEMENT:

Definition-

In the words of Henry Fayol, "To manage is to forecast and to plan, to organize, to command, to co-ordinate and to control".

According to Peter F Drucker, "Management is a multi-purpose organ that manages a business and manages managers and manages worker and work".

In the words of J.N. Schulze, "Management is the force which leads, guides, and directs an organization in the accomplishment of a pre-determined object".

In the words of Koontz and O'Donnel, "Management is defined as the creation and maintenance of an internal environment in an enterprise where individuals working together in groups can perform efficiently and effectively towards the attainment of group goals".

Management simple means to control or to administer. Office management is the method of controlling an office to achieve a given aim. In our modern society, all kinds of business are carried on by a group of people with adequate knowledge in their respective filed. However, a group of people working for a common object must be guided and controlled by a leader or an authority. This is the function of the management. Management is a technique of leadership or control of an office in order to attain the aimed result through the efforts of other people in grouped activities. This is possible only when the office is properly organized and managed. Office function is carried on by a group of people for a common result, by giving services to the organization. The management has to organize the office in such a way to attain the objectives. It is the function of the management to organize, guide, and control the activities of the office personnel. That is why in the present era, personnel management has become a specialized subject.

An analysis of the various definitions of management indicates that management has certain characteristics. The following are the salient characteristics of management:

- **Management aims at reaping rich results in economic terms**: Manager's primary task is to secure the productive performance through planning, direction, and control. The management is expected to bring in the desired results. Rational utilization of available resources to maximize the profit is the economic function of a manager. A professional manager can prove his administrative talent by smartly using resources and enhancing profit. According to Kimball, "Management is the art of applying the economic principles that underlie the control of men and materials in the enterprise under consideration".

- **Management also implies skill and experience in getting things done through people:** Management is a people- involving job. Profitable returns cannot be expected without enlisting cooperation and securing positive response from "people". Hiring ones with specialized expertise is the significant aspect of the management. In the words of Koontz and O'Donnell, "Management is the art of getting things done through people in formally organized groups".

- **Management is a process:** Management is a process, function or activity. This process continues until the objectives set by administration are actually achieved. "Management is a social process involving coordination of human and material resources through the functions of planning, organizing, staffing, leading, and controlling in order to accomplish stated objectives".

- **Management is a universal activity:** Management does not apply to business undertakings only. It is applicable to political, social, religious and educational institutions as well. Management is necessary when group effort is required.

- **Management is a science as well as an art:** Management is an art because there are definite principles of management. It is also a science because by the application of these principles, predetermined objectives can be achieved.

- **Management is a profession:** Management is gradually becoming a profession because there are established principles of management being applied in practice, involves specialized training and is governed by ethical code arising out of its social obligations.

- **Management is an endeavor to achieve predetermined objectives:** Management is concerned with directing and controlling of the various activities of the organization to attain the predetermined objectives. Every managerial activity has certain objectives. Management deals particularly with the actual directing of human efforts.

- **Management is a group activity:** Management comes into existence only when there is a group activity towards a common objective. Management is always concerned with group efforts and not individual efforts. To achieve the goals of an organization, management- plans, organizes, coordinates, directs, and controls the group effort.

- **Management is a system of authority:** Authority means power to make others act in a predetermined manner. Management formalizes a standard set of rules and procedure to be followed by the subordinates and ensures their compliance with the rules and regulations. Since management is a process of directing men to perform a task, the authority to extract the work from others is implied in the very concept of management.

- **Management involves decision-making**: Management implies making decisions regarding the organization and operation of business in different dimensions. The success or failure of an organization can be judged by the quality of decisions taken by the managers. Therefore, decisions are key to the performance of a manager.
- **Management implies good leadership**: A manager must have the ability to lead and get the desired course of action from the subordinates. According to R. C. Davis, "Management is the function of executive leadership everywhere". Management of the high order implies the capacity of managers to influence the behavior of their subordinates.
- **Management is dynamic and not static**: The principles of management are dynamic and not static. It has to adapt itself according to social changes.
- **Management draws ideas and concepts from various disciplines**: Management is an interdisciplinary study. It draws ideas and concepts from various disciplines like economics, statistics, mathematics, psychology, sociology, anthropology, etc.
- **Management is goal-oriented**: Management is a purposeful activity. It is concerned with notes and the achievement of predetermined objectives of an organization.
- **Different levels of management**: Management is needed at different levels of an organization namely top level, middle level, and lower level.
- **Need of organization**: There is the need of an organizational setup for the success of management. Management uses the organization for achieving pre-determined objectives.
- **Management need not be owners**: Managers don't need to be the owners of the enterprise. In joint-stock companies, management and owners (capital) are different entities.
- **Management is intangible**: It cannot be seen with the eyes. It is evident only through the quality of the organization and their results, i.e., profits, increased productivity, etc.

Before trying to understand management, it is essential to understand the meaning and definition of administration which is as follows:

Administration concerns determination of corporate policy, coordination of finance, production and distribution, settlement of the organization's compass and the ultimate control of the executive.

According to schedule, "Administration is the force which lays down the object for which an organization and its management are to strive and the broad polices under which they are to operate. Management is the force which leads guides and directs an organization in the accomplishment of a predetermined object. Organization is the combination of the necessary human beings, materials, tools, equipment, working space and appurtenances, brought together in systematic and effective correlation, to accomplish some desired object."

According to Milward, "Administration is primarily the process, an agency used to establish the object or purpose which an undertaking and its staff are to achieve. Secondarily, administration has to plan and stabilize the broad lines or principles which will govern the action. These broad lines are in their turn, usually called policies. Management is the process and the agency through which the execution of policy is planned and supervised. Organization is the process of dividing work into convenient tasks or duties, of grouping such duties in the form of posts of delegating authority to each post and of appointing qualified staff to be responsible that the work is carried out as planned."

It is known through economics that the factors of production are divided into four- land, labour, capital and entrepreneur. The last one is important under the present study. The entrepreneur is the man who brings together the other factors in a business. The other factors can be called as an organization. For example- consider a human body. The human body can be compared as an organization. It has various organs- ears to hear, eyes to see, hands to work, legs to walk, etc. Each organ has a specific work. Each of the organs works in coordination with the other organs. All the activities of the different organs combined can be considered as an organization. Finally, there is a top administrator i.e. the brain. Similarly, in business, production department, sales department, personnel department, etc have to do the proper function as directed by the management. The organization may refer to the function of organization or plans carried out through persons. Organization is concerned with and exists when an employee is selected, assigned jobs within his ability to work through a clear understanding. He must understand what he should do, how he should do and when he should do.

Office administration denotes the function of giving birth to major policies on which the enterprise is to be functioned. In a joint- stock company, the Board of Directors makes the major policies and in a partnership firm, partners lay down the policies. In all kinds of business, the function of administration is the same. Making policies is the function of administration.

PRINCIPLES OF MANAGEMENT:

1. **Division of Work:** In practice, employees are specialized in different areas and they have different skills. Different levels of expertise can be distinguished within the knowledge areas (from generalist to specialist). Personal and professional developments support this. According to Henri Fayol, specialization promotes the efficiency of the workforce and increases productivity. Moreover, specialization of the workforce increases their accuracy and speed. This management principle of the fourteen principles of management is applicable to both technical and managerial activities.

2. **Authority and Responsibility:** In order to get things done in an organization, management has the authority to give orders to the employees. Of course, with this authority comes responsibility. According to Henri Fayol, the accompanying power or authority gives the management the right to give orders to the subordinates. The responsibility can be traced back from performance, and it is therefore, necessary to make agreements about this. In other words, authority, and responsibility go together and they are two sides of the same coin.

3. **Discipline:** This third principle of the fourteen principles of management is about obedience. It is often a part of the core values of a mission and vision in the form of good conduct and respectful interactions. This management principle is essential and is seen as the oil to make the engine of an organization run smoothly.

4. **Unity of Command:** The management principle 'Unity of command' means that an individual employee should receive orders from the manager and that the employee is answerable to that manager. If tasks

and related responsibilities are given to the employee by more than one manager, this may lead to confusion which may lead to possible conflicts for employees. By using this principle, the responsibility for mistakes can be established more easily.

5. **Unity of Direction**: This management principle of the fourteen principles of management is all about focus and unity. All employees deliver the same activities that can be linked to the same objectives. All activities must be carried out by one group that forms a team. These activities must be described in a plan of action. The manager is ultimately responsible for this plan, and he monitors the progress of the defined and planned activities. Focus areas are the efforts made by the employees and coordination.

6. **Subordination of Individual Interest**: There are always all kinds of interests in an organization. In order to have an organization function well, Henri Fayol indicated that personal interests are subordinate to the interests of the organization (ethics). The primary focus is on the organizational objectives and not on those of the individual. This applies to all levels of the entire organization, including the managers.

7. **Remuneration**: Motivation and productivity are close to one another as far as the smooth running of an organization is concerned. This management principle of the 14 principles of management argues that the remuneration should be sufficient to keep employees motivated and productive. There are two types of remuneration namely non- monetary (a compliment, more responsibilities, credits) and monetary (compensation, bonus or other financial compensation). Ultimately, it is about rewarding the efforts that have been made.

8. **The Degree of Centralization**: Management and authority for decision-making process must be properly balanced in an organization. This depends on the volume and size of an organization including its hierarchy. Centralization implies the concentration of decision-making authority at the top management (executive board). Sharing of authorities for the decision-making process with lower levels (middle and lower management), is referred to as decentralization by Henri Fayol. Henri Fayol indicated that an organization should strive for a good balance in this.

9. **Scalar Chain**: Hierarchy presents itself in any given organization. This varies from senior management (executive board) to the lowest levels in the organization. Henri Fayol's "hierarchy" management principle states

that there should be a clear line in the area of authority (from top to bottom and all managers at all levels). This can be seen as a type of management structure. Each employee can contact a manager or a superior in an emergency situation without challenging the hierarchy. Especially when it concerns reports about calamities to the immediate managers/superiors.

10. **Order:** According to this principle of the 14 principles of management, employees in an organization must have the right resources at their disposal so that they can function properly in an organization. In addition to social order (responsibility of the managers) the work environment must be safe, clean and tidy.

11. **Equity**: The management principle of equity often occurs in the core values of an organization. According to Henri Fayol, employees must be treated kindly and equally. Employees must be in the right place in the organization to do things right. Managers should supervise and monitor this process and they should treat employees fairly and impartially.

12. **Stability of Tenure of Personnel:** This management principle of the fourteen principles of management represents deployment and managing of personnel and which should be in balance with the service that is provided from the organization. Management strives to minimize employee turnover and have the right staff at the right place. Focus areas such as frequent change of position and sufficient development must be managed well.

13. **Initiative:** Henri Fayol argued that with this management principle, employees should be allowed to express new ideas. This encourages interest and involvement and creates added value for the company. Employee initiatives are a source of strength for the organization according to Henri Fayol. This encourages the employees to be involved and interested.

14. **Esprit de Corps**: The management principle 'esprit de corps' of the fourteen principles of management stands for striving for the involvement and unity of the employees. Managers are responsible for the development of morale in the workplace; individually and in the area of communication. Esprit de corps contributes to the development of the culture and creates an atmosphere of mutual trust and understanding.

The fourteen principles of management can be used to manage organizations and are useful tools for forecasting, planning, process management, organization management, decision- making, coordination, and control. Although they are obvious, many of these matters are still used based on common sense in current management practices in organizations. It remains a practical list with focus areas that are based on Henri Fayol's research which still applies today due to a number of logical principles.

ELEMENTS OF OFFICE MANAGEMENT

Elements of office management are termed as pillars of a building. If the pillars are strong, certainly, the building is also strong. Hence, efficient functioning of office management is based on the elements of office management. Following are the essential elements of office management.

a. **Personnel**: Office personnel are responsible for the official work within an organization. Generally, the selection and placement of office personnel is carried on by the office manager in small organizations. In large organization, staffing is carried out by the human resource management department. In both the case, the office work is to be performed by allocating the work to each individual according to their efficiency, guide the personnel to do the work with the help of means available in an office within a specified time and control the activities of office personnel. The office manager has to do all these activities.

b. **Means**: Means refers to tools used to perform office work. Means include pen, pencil, eraser, paper, ink, office forms, typewriter, computer, printer, calculator, etc. Adequate tools need to be supplied in an office and put them to the most efficient and economical use for achieving objectives.

c. **Environment**: The nature of business determines the environment of an office. The various office works have to be carried under a particular condition or environment. A work environment is created and maintained for the smooth performance of office work. It is the duty and responsibility of an office manager to bring suitable environment by adopting various procedures and practice.

d. **Purpose**: The office personnel must be aware of the purpose of work is and the impact of such work on other's performance. The office manager teaches the purpose to office personnel. If not done, the economical and justifiable use of resources and the objectives of the organization cannot be realized.

FUNCTIONS OF MANAGEMENT:

There is no universally acceptance to the classification of management functions. This is because different authors considering different organizations give a separate classification of management functions. Office management is similar to general or administrative management and performs the same functions as are performed by the management. The functions of office management in brief, are given below:

1. <u>Planning</u>

Planning is a fundamental function of office management. All types of organizations prepare plans. Planning our studies, careers, new products, etc are examples of planning. Determination of a course of action determines the achievement of a desired result. Planning concentrates on setting and achieving objectives of an organization. It is an intellectual process. It is characterized as the process of thinking before doing. Planning function of management precedes all other managerial functions. "Planning is deciding in advance what is to be done. When a manager plans, he projects a course of action for the future, attempting to achieve a consistent, coordinated structure of operations aimed at the desired results." Planning involves projecting the future course of action for the business as a whole and also for different sections within it. Planning is thus the preparatory step for actions and helps in bridging the gap between the present and the future. Since planning is essentially choosing, it is dependent upon the availability of alternatives. It is through this process of choosing that office manager can obviously be seen as an important aspect of planning. Planning process comprises determination and lying down of objectives, policies, procedures, rules, programmes, budget and strategies, etc. The operations of the office will not run smoothly if they are not planned adequately. Planning makes it possible to occur which would not otherwise happen.

<u>Benefits of Planning:</u>

• The business objectives can easily be secured through plans.

- Planning gives direction to activities in the office.
- It focuses attention on objectives.
- It provides coordinated efforts and reduces risk and uncertainties.
- It facilitates the process of decision-making.
- It encourages innovation and creativity.
- It serves as a basis of control.
- It encourages a sense of involvement and team spirit.
- It eliminates unproductive office work and thus helps to minimize cost.
- It helps in economical operations.

2. <u>Organizing</u>

It is an important managerial activity through which management brings together the human and material resources for the achievement of certain objectives. Organization is the foundation upon which the whole structure of management is built. It may be conceived as the structuring of functions and duties to be performed by a group of people for the purpose of attaining enterprise objectives. Organizing is determining, grouping and arranging of the various activities, assigning of people to those activities, providing of suitable physical factors of environment and the indicating of the relative authority delegated to each individual charged with the execution of each respective activity.

According to Louis A Allen, "Organization is the process of identifying and grouping the work to be performed, defining and delegating responsibility and authority, and establishing relationships for the purpose of enabling people to work most effectively together in accomplishing objectives."

According to Liver Sheldon, "Organization is the process of combining the work which individuals and groups have to perform with the faculties necessary for its execution that the duties so formed provide the best channels for efficient, systematic, positive and coordinated application of the available effort."

<u>Steps of Organization:</u>

The important steps involved in the process of an organization are:

- **Identification of Activities** An organizational structure is developed to achieve objectives. Organization as a process of management is concerned with identifying and grouping of activities to be performed.

- **Grouping of Activities**: Closely related and similar activities are grouped together to form departments, divisions or sections. The grouping may be done on several bases depending on the requirements of the situation. Such grouping of activities is called departmentation.

- **Assignment of Duties**: Each group of related activities is assigned a position most suited for it. Every position is occupied by an individual. While assigning duties, the requirements of the job and the competence of the individual are matched together. The process of assigning duties goes on till the last level of the organization.

- **Delegation of Authority**: Authority without responsibility is a dangerous likewise; responsibility without authority is an empty vessel. Hence, corresponding to the responsibility, authority is delegated to the sub-ordinates enabling them to show work performance.

- **Fitting Individuals**: Having determined the various parts and portions of the job to be done, the next step will be to fix suitable and well-qualified persons into these activities. Each person in the group will be given a specific part of the job to do and will be made responsible for it.

3. <u>Staffing</u>

'Staffing' is concerned with the recruitment, selection, placement, training, growth and development of all those members of the organization whose function is to get things done through the efforts of other individuals. After determining the number and type of personnel to be appointed to fill different jobs, management starts recruiting, selecting the training the people to fulfil the requirements of the enterprise. According to Franklin Moore, "Staffing is a forward-looking activity because tomorrow keeps becoming today. Attrition constantly reduces executive ranks through retirement, death, resignations and occasional dismissal; so young men keep moving up. Besides this, most enterprises grow, providing new openings for managers." The function of staffing was considered to be a part of organizing but recently it has developed into a distinct function of management, and is, therefore treated separately in the chapter relating to Personnel Management.

4. <u>Directing</u>

Once plans are drawn up to re-determine the objectives and the organization is ready to go into action, competent people/staff are appointed. Directing is the managerial function of guiding, inspiring, instructing and harnessing people towards the accomplishment of desired results. It is that part of the management process, which actuates the members of an organization to work effectively and efficiently for the achievement of the goals. Koentz and Q 'donnel defined direction as, "The interpersonal aspect of managing aimed at achieving the enterprise's objectives through understanding and effective contribution of the subordinates." According to Haimann, "Directing consists of the process and techniques utilized in issuing instructions and making certain that operations are carried on as originally planned. Directing is around which all performance revolves. It is the essence of operations, and coordination is a necessary by-product of good managerial directing." Directing consists of the following steps:

- Issuing orders and instructions to the sub-ordinates.
- Guiding and teaching the proper method of work to the sub-ordinates.
- Supervising the work of sub-ordinates to ensure that it conforms to the plan.
- Motivation of the sub-ordinates by providing incentives.

5. <u>Motivating</u>

The term motivation has been derived from the word motive. Motive is anything that initiates or sustains activity. It is an inner state that energizes, activates or moves and directs or channels behavior towards goals. Motive is a psychological force within an individual that sets him in motion. Behind every human action, there is a motive. According to Brech, "Motivation is a general inspirational process which gets the members of the team to pull their weight effectively, to give their loyalty to the group, carry out the accepted task properly and play an effective part in the job that the group has undertaken." The important task of office management is to motivate employees to direct their efforts towards the accomplishment of organizational goals. Motivating may be achieved by: Providing inducements and incentives to employees, keeping morals high, satisfying the needs of the employees, etc.

6. <u>Co-coordinating</u>

Along with specialization, there must be conscious efforts on the part of the management to see that all activities carried on by experts and different departments, contribute to the achievement of the objective of the business. Smooth working of an enterprise and the achievement of its objectives depend on sound co-ordination. According to Lundy, "Co-ordination involves the development of unity of purpose and the harmonious implementation of plans for the achievement of desired ends." According to Mooney and Reiley coordination is the, "Orderly arrangement of group efforts to provide the unit of action in pursuit of a common purpose." Thus coordination may be achieved by:

- Simplified organization.
- Harmonized programmes and policies.
- Well-designed method of communication.
- Voluntary cooperation.
- Coordination through supervision.
- Clear-cut objectives.
- Clear definition of authority and responsibility.
- Effective leadership.

7. <u>Controlling</u>

"To control is to determine what is being accomplished; that is to evaluate performance and, if necessary, to apply corrective measures so that performance takes place according to the plans. After the plans are put into action, there can be several hurdles in the achievement goals. Results may fall short of targets. Direction may be faulty. Therefore, management must find out what is going wrong, what changes in plans and directions are required and what must be done to set things right. This is the function of control. In words of Anthony "Management control is the process by which managers assure that resources are obtained and used effectively and efficiently in the accomplishment of an organization's objectives." The basic elements of the control process:

- Establishment of standards or objectives.
- Measurements of actual performance.

- Comparing actual performance against the standard set.
- Determining the reason for deviation.
- Taking corrective action.
- Feedback.

Control is thus closely related to the planning job of the manager. Nevertheless, it should not be viewed merely as a post-mortem of past achievements and performance. In practice, a good control system should suggest corrective measures so that negative deviations may not recur in future.

8. <u>Communication</u>

Communication is a means by which different persons are linked together in a group or organization to attain a common goal. No group activity is possible without communication. It enables the members to coordinate, exchange and make progress. A good communication must aim at making everyone concerned aware of the goal which the organization wants to achieve.

The two main objectives of communication are to inform and persuade. Communication is the means by which behavior is modified, change is affected, and goals are achieved. Communication is essential for effective control and motivation.

SUCCESS RULES FOR OFFICE MANAGERS:

In any office environment, the office manager acts as the glue that holds a team together. While the duties of the position may vary depending on the specific line of work, a keen sense of leadership and the well-being of the team should guide the office manager's mission. This role is absolutely crucial to the overall success of an office, which is why we've outlined six useful tips for office managers, working in any field, on how to be more successful at their job.

1. **Establish Goals for Your Team-**

Establishing clear office goals will create a sense of purpose that drives your team forward and keeps them productive and motivated. Inspire your team members to create ambitious yet achievable personal goals that reflect their work values and benefit the rest of the workforce. The sense of fulfillment that comes with accomplishing a goal will motivate employees to continue excelling, and you'll be able to better monitor their progress by knowing what exactly they are working toward.

2. Communication is Key

It's the office manager's responsibility to unify a workplace, which means establishing straightforward and open communication between the members of your team. Ensure that they know their specific duties and give them constructive feedback when helpful or necessary. Teach your team members to clearly articulate their needs and actively listen to one another so that no one is in the dark about what is expected of them. There are many moving parts in any given office environment, and it's the office manager's responsibility to implement clear methods of communication to ensure those parts are working together productively.

3. A Little Bit of Fun Goes a Long Way

No matter the kind of office environment you foster as a manager, you should always make room for occasional fun. Whether that means putting in extra effort to make the holiday party better than last year, setting aside weekly team bonding time, or a gesture as simple as implementing casual dress Fridays, keep in mind that happy employees are hardworking employees. Moreover, getting to know the members of your team outside of a work environment can strengthen personal relationships, in turn, benefit the workplace productivity.

4. Know Your Boundaries

While it's crucial to show the members of your team a more candid side of your personality, it's equally important to maintain boundaries separating your work life and personal life. You want to cultivate a comfortable work environment without blurring the lines of acceptable workplace conduct. Remind the people in your office that you are their friend, but not their best friend.

5. Be an Office Role Model

As the office manager, you should serve as a role model for the members of your team. At the end of the day, the only behavior you can control is your own, which means it's up to you to lead by example and embody the workplace values that you wish to see reflected throughout the office. Show them how far a little bit of positivity can go in boosting team morale or getting through a particularly hard day. Uplift and embolden your team when struggles arise and treat everyone with the respect they deserve. After enough time, your example will become the standard.

6. Go the Extra Mile

Within the complex machine of an office, there are some things bound to fall through the cracks, and it should be the office manager who provides the extra hand. Show your team members that you are willing to make sacrifices that enrich the office environment and make their work lives more enjoyable. Stay late when there's extra work that needs to get done, and if you can manage it, offer to take work off someone's hands if you see they are drowning in deadlines. If you continue to go above and beyond, you should find that your team will gladly meet you halfway.

Qualities of a successful office manager-

- **Leadership:** A good office manager must possess the quality of leading the office staff rather than driving them. Although leadership ability is inherent, it can be developed by training and experience.
- **Sound Judgment:** Sound judgment is required under two circumstances (a) Whether the person whom the work is to be delegated and has the ability to do the work (b) In dealing with disciplinary matters with workers.
- **Impartially:** The office manager must treat his staff impartially in order to gain their confidence and respect.
- **Shrewdness:** This quality refers to the ability to deal with a situation and to take appropriate action.

- **Courage**: This implies backing the shrewdness by courage. He should not contradict his own judgment.
- **Methodical:** This quality implies the orderly performance of office work. He must organize the work of his staff systematically.
- **Good Character:** An office manager must stand firm to his decisions. However, firmness should not be taken to mean stubbornness.
- **Forward Looking:** An office manager must keep himself up to date in relation to office system, methods and techniques so as to improve the efficiency of the office.
- **Personal Qualities:** Personal qualities of an office manager are a combination of personal traits such as honesty, sincerely, initiative, self-discipline, punctuality, humorous, tact, persuasiveness and an attractive personality.
- **Professional interests:** In addition to the usual knowledge in the field of office management, an office manager must also have interest in professional fields such as Management Science, Cost Accountancy, Financial Management, Secretarial Procedure, knowledge relating to law and so on. These professional interests make him become a wholesome office manager.

FUNCTIONS OF OFFICE MANAGERS:

Each office has a personality of its own. This personality is a reflection of the purpose for which an office exists. The manufacturing office will have a profile that differs from that of the sales office. The accounting office will have a different orientation from that of a research and development office. In organizing a new office, the office manager must first determine the prime reason of the existence of that office and then add the necessary ingredients to bring about an efficient operation entity that achieves predetermined results: Although, offices differ from one another in prime responsibility, many activities are commonly carried out by all the offices. Some of these activities are:

- Processing incoming mail.
- Processing outgoing mail.
- Maintenance of records (Filing and Indexing).

- Establishing standard at office work.
- Designing and procuring at office forms, stationery, etc.
- Recruitment and training of office staff.
- Maintenance of furniture, machines, appliances, etc.
- Preparation of statements, reports, etc.
- Maintenance of accounts and other financial records.
- Handling Telephone calls and enquiries.
- Preparing updated information for the whole firm.
- Arranging the data in a quick and accessible form for use.
- Safeguarding the assets.
- Keeping prompt and accurate handling of enquiries orders.
- Maintaining an efficient flow of work in the office.

Some broad functions of the office managers-

a. **Leadership:** An office manager has to control his office. He/She is important for the smooth running of an organization. He is in-charge of the public relations. He helps other departments to achieve their goals. He has complete control over the work done in the office.

b. **Coordination:** He has to select the persons- right persons for the right jobs.

    i. He will have to work and carefully see that the policies laid down by the management are implemented.

    ii. He is the connecting link between the top management and the workers. Workers approach him for their grievances and difficulties and the manager has to redress them. If he is not able to do the needful, he must place it before the management.

    iii. He has to work and safeguard the firm, where he is an office manager.

    iv. His primary duty is to the management and secondary duty to the workers. He must please both the parties. If either one of the parties is annoyed or neglected, he will be regarded as a bad manager.

c. **Recruitment of Staff:** He has to select the right person for the right job. For that he invites applications, conducts interviews and selects personnel.

d. **Training of Staff:** He provides training to the new employees as well as old employees to improve their skill in the latest techniques of management.

e. **Motivation:** He measures the employees work and output and offers rewards which increase their efficiency and ensure their better cooperation and lead to the promotion of the staff.

f. **Discipline:** Discipline in the office depends upon him. The sub ordinates should follow the rules and principles of management. He must have ability to speak. New methods cannot be accepted, unless full explanation is followed. He has to convince others about the fact findings.

g. **Accounting:** He has to keep a close touch with the accounting and costing section.

h. **Controls Stationary:** He has to safeguard the furniture, fittings, machines, equipments and various types of records.

a. **Secretarial Services:** He maintains statutory and accounts books, holds meetings, drafts report and minutes, etc. Thus, he does the secretary's functions.

j. **Organizer and Supervisor:** He organizes and supervises the office correspondence, messenger services, communication system, filling and indexing, protection of records, etc. There is no hard and fast rule as to the functions of an office manager. His functions depend upon the type and size of the organization.

POINTS TO REMEMBER:

- Management is defined as the creation and maintenance of an internal environment in an enterprise where individuals working together in groups can perform efficiently and effectively towards the attainment of group goals.
- Management also implies skill and experience in getting things done through people.
- Management is a science as well as an art.
- Management works on fourteen principles.

- Management functions are: Planning, Organizing, Staffing, Directing, Motivating, Coordinating, Controlling and Communication.
- The functions of an office manager are: Leadership, Coordination, Recruitment, Training and Motivation.

GLOSSARY:

- **Management**: Process of controlling and making decisions about an organization, as well as overseeing others to ensure activities are performed efficiently and effectively.
- **Planning**: Process of setting goals and objectives and deciding how to accomplish them.
- **Organization**: Body of people that come together for a specific purpose.
- **Staffing**: Process of recruiting, hiring, training, evaluating, and compensating employees.
- **Controlling**: Continuous process of comparing actual outcomes with planned outcomes and taking corrective measures when goals are not met.
- **Authority**: Power to carry out a task and make decisions.
- **Motivation**: Force that inspires employees to want to perform their best and achieve results.
- **Unity of Command:** States that each employee reports to one manager.
- **Leadership**: Ability to influence others to reach a goal.
- **Communication:** Skill by which different persons are linked together in a group or organization to attain a common goal.

CHAPTER THREE

MAILING SERVICES

INTRODUCTION

The history of mail or messaging services extends messages from one place to another, starting with the invention of writing. The first documented use of the postal system occurred in Egypt around 2400 BCE when Faros used officials to send instructions throughout the empire. The same type of courier service may have been used in the Fertile Crescent (500- 220 BCE), the Han Dynasty in China (306 BCE) - 221 CE), the Islamic State (622-1923) CE) in Arabia, the Inca empire in Peru (1250-1550 CE), and the Mughal Empire in India (1650- 1857 CE). Learners must be aware of the postal services, generally used to send letter/posts manually through government postal department. This may take long time or few days to deliver the post.

Nowadays, mailing services to send and receive the text, photo, etc have been changed into electronic mail. Electronic mail is a technique of exchanging messages between people using electronic gadgets. It was founded by Ray Tomlinson in 1972 named as email or e-mail. It works on all computer networks which is called Internet. Sending this electronic post distance between the sender and receiver does not matter. Earlier email programs required the sender and recipient to both be online at the same time for instant messaging. Today's advanced email servers need not be online at the same time. These servers are quite able to send, receive and store the messages. Users or their computers need not be online at the same time; they need to connect briefly, usually to a mail server or web interface as long as it takes sending or receiving messages or downloading them. Even today's mobile device has made it very easy to send and receive the mail anytime, anywhere.

INCOMING AND OUTGOING MAILS

What do you mean by mail?

'Mail' means a written communication via a messenger service or post office. All business concerns send and receive large amounts of letters, notices, circulars, calls, reminder reports, statements, pamphlets, queries, etc. The postal service ensures continuous communication between internal and external parties. It assists the firm in establishing and maintaining communication with customers, suppliers, and other stakeholders.

In order to ensure prompt postal management, the postal service must be organized and systematized. Because of its importance and the important role played in the organization, email should receive special attention. In companies, mail handling is done by a special department called Mailing department. The type of order of the mail delivery department depends on the size of the firm and the amount of mail to be handled. Generally, a mail is categorized as incoming mail, outgoing mail and the communication between different departments of the same company called inter-departmental mail. Email refers to the communication between the parties through electronic gadgets. This requires an electronic setup.

Managing incoming mails-

Good mail management requires the establishment of a thorough process that includes step by step email management. Incoming mail should be received and communicated with speed and accuracy. The exact way to handle internal mail varies from office to office. Managing incoming mail usually consists of the following steps.

- **Acceptance of mail:** The post is sent once or twice a day by post or courier. When a mailbox or mail bag is rented, mail is collected by an employee from the post office once or twice a day. The clerk is assigned the task of receiving letters and issuing receipts or notifying them that he or she has received them from the peon / messenger's letter.
- **Mail opening:** Letters are opened by hand or by machine. Mail must be opened carefully to ensure mail security. It should also be noted that there are no papers left inside the envelope. The chief executive officer must handle this process.
- **Content Evaluation:** The contents of envelopes should be examined to determine the purpose of communication with the department concerned. If there are enclosed areas, they should be inspected to make sure they are in order. Any discrepancies should be brought to the notice of the postal manager, especially where the entry is by check, written, postal orders, etc.
- **Stamp closure:** After opening the mail, each letter must be in writing on the date and time of receipt. The stamp can be made by rubber stamp, by hand or with the help of dating, counting and time recording machines. If necessary, the envelope should be pinned as proof. The letter is marked to the department concerned and a circulation slip, if needed.
- **Recording:** Details of the letters received are recorded on the 'Internal Mail Record' or 'Books Received' or any register. It ensures that the letters are not lost or remain neglected but it is time consuming when the mail is large.
- **Categorization and supply:** Letters are sorted into trays or baskets or cabinets in the pigeon's den and sent to the appropriate departments. Finding a clerk is signing a list or registering as an adoption.

Managing outgoing mails-

Almost all offices send mail daily. Outgoing mail must be handled with care because the speed and accuracy of managing such mails play a vital role. The following reasons demand the careful management of the mails:

- Improper handling of external mail creates a negative impression on third parties.

- A delay in submitting responses may result in a loss of business opportunities.
- Delays may incur additional costs.

<u>All outgoing mail goes through three stages:</u>

[i] Forming a mail [ii] Signing over mail [iii] Recording of mail

Forming includes writing or dictation as well as typing (or writing) of a draft or reported item. Standard letters may be signed by the new staff on behalf of the principal but the important letters are signed by the official or the head concerned. Only an authorized person must sign over the official letter/ post. After that, every letter should be written up with a code or file number for future reference. This process is known as a reference. Each organization follows its own code-and-expression method, e.g. the reference number UOU/ Exam/06/2020 indicates that letter No.06 pertaining to the exam department was filed in 2020.

Manage inter-departmental mails-

At large organizations, all mails of the department are handled almost exactly the same as the one described above. A separate register may be maintained for the central departmental mails but for smaller organizations, this can be handled simply by mentioning a letter of the book or letters of the messengers.

<u>FUNDAMENTAL ACTIVITIES OF MAIL HANDLING DEPARTMENT:</u>

Managing external mail usually involves the following steps:

1. **Collection of outgoing mails:** Usually, each department sends its letters to the email department for mailing. In some offices, a messenger from the post office travels at scheduled times to collect mail from various departments. The tray marked as 'outgoing mail' is kept in each department. All letters to be exported are placed in the tray and the messenger collects the email from that tray. Timely collection of outgoing mail improves the efficiency of the batch phase.

2. **Mail Entry:** Maintain records of all the mail is the primary duty of the mail handling department Letters to be delivered locally by courier or by peon are recorded in the messenger book. Entries are placed in the Outgoing Mail Register or Dispatch Register.

3. **Creasing of the letter:** The letter should be carefully folded and in the correct size. The texture should be precise and should not damage the solitude of the characters. They should be grouped into a minimum number of folders. When a windows envelope is used, the wrap should be done in such a way the address can be seen through a window. Standard envelopes should be used to accommodate letters. Before letters are placed in envelopes, you should take care:

- Write the number of letters in the envelope and in the letter, itself as listed in the dispatch register.
- Also, look at the entries as mentioned at the bottom left of the book.
- Add the enclosures with pins, tags, clips, or strings.

Nowadays, machines are used to wrap letters and place them in envelopes automatically.

1. **Preparation of envelopes:** After wrapping, the letters are placed in the appropriate envelopes. A complete and correct address must be provided. Pin codes should be provided as they guarantee faster delivery. The address is written on the letter and the envelope must accompany the message. A windows envelope is used to prevent the rewriting of an address in an envelope. The address must be fully identifiable by hand or in writing. Speech machines can be used whenever needed. The envelopes should be sealed with a gum, paste or cello tape. The work is tedious but must be done with care. The sticker should not spread internally, as it can damage the content. Various mail categories, such as 'Book Post', 'Registered Post' should be mentioned over the envelope.

2. **Sorting, measuring and stamping:** The envelope for the different mail categories should be arranged in phases. External mail is usually in two categories-(i) Domestic (ii) Outstation

The second category can be classified as standard postal mail, registered, speed, postal mail, foreign mail, under shipping certificate, Indian Airlines, Air India, sea mail, etc. The mail must be typed in separate ports so that the stamp function is enabled. Stamps should be posted on postage. It is necessary to measure the different articles that will be mailed to the appropriate number of stamps. A timely copy of the 'Post Office Guide' should be kept with the Dispatch clerk responsible for the postage stamps. In large organizations, filtering machines are used for treading. Letters to be sent by courier are included in the messenger or peon book and forwarded to the courier for distribution.

3. Delivery: Finally, shipping and delivery of books must be organized. Regular mail is posted at the nearest post box from time to time. Special types of mail such as subscriptions and insurance, etc are sent by post separately.

Handling E-Mail-

Electronic mail or E-mail is the fastest and easiest way to send messages, data, graphics etc. over the Internet. You know that the Internet is a worldwide network of computers connected by satellite. To receive and send emails online you need to have an email address. E-mail are usually received and sent by the concerned authority. In the case of senior officials, the job is assigned to their assistant or secretary.

While sending emails, one must be very careful as it is not possible to correct the original message once it is forwarded. Another important thing is that a hard copy of the message must be kept on file as proof.

FILING SYSTEM:

As a primary source of information, all records in the office need to be kept for future reference. Completion serves the purpose of keeping records in all offices. Documents and papers are filed and available on demand. Completion is the process of arranging the records in the correct order for easy access. Captioning can be defined as the process of editing and maintaining original records or copies, so that they can be easily found where they are needed. It involves the installation of documents in standard containers in a predetermined format so that any document can be obtained quickly and correctly when needed.

The main purposes of the filling process are to ensure proper ordering, proper storage and easy access to records. The active filing system is expected to have the following objectives:

- Cataloging and unifying records.
- To protect documents from loss or damage.
- Providing easy access to information without wasting time.
- Availability of past records to future business policy managers and agencies.

Functions of the filing system:

The functions of the filing system are as follows:

- Storage of file covers or folders in cupboard-mounted cabinets.
- Issuance of files filed in any department.
- Transfers of papers no longer used from existing files to separate folders or box files for future use.
- Completion of letters and other documents after the action taken on the cover of the cardboard file or folders.
- Classification of documents on a predetermined basis.
- Disposal of no longer applicable old papers and records.

<u>CLASSIFICATION OF FILING:</u>

Documentation is required to ensure immediate access to records. Separation is a process of selecting subjects for which records and documents are organized due to general characteristics prior to completion. For example, characters can be separated on the basis of a communication issue. The main arrangements for file classification in the office are:

- Serial from 1-100
- Serial from A-Z
- Geographical
- According to the title

1. **Serial from 1-100**

Under this technique, files are arranged numerically, each link or subject is assigned a number. The files are arranged in numerical order. For example, a customer, XYZ, may be assigned No.06 so that all related papers are available in folder no. 06.

2. Serial from A-Z

With this technique, letters from different groups or related to different topics are organized and placed in different file covers on the basis of the alphabet on which the group's name or subject begins. The first alphabet of a name or surname or title is the first directory of the file rank. For example, all documents related to Tata Consultancies can be placed in a folder marked T'. For each file, the papers are sorted by date.

3. Geographical subdivision

In the technique, books are subdivided according to geographical areas. All connections related to a specific location are stored in one file.

4. According to the title

Under this technique, papers are organized according to the topic. Subjects are listed alphabetically, e.g. Exam, Result, Study material, etc. This method is more appropriate if the title is more important than the author's name or location.

Methods of filing-

After classification, files should be carefully stored using any of the appropriate filing methods. There are various ways to fill them based on the type of equipment they use. These methods can be classified as-(i) Traditional Methods (ii) Modern Methods

1. Traditional Filing Methods

There are some traditional methods of filing such as pigeon-hole installation, folder filing, box placement, spike filing, book bind filing, and arch lever filing. Although, these filing systems have limited use nowadays, these do apply to smaller organizations. These methods can be defined as:

a. **Pigeon cave installation-** It is a special almirah or wardrobe divided by the number of smaller areas. It is open from one side and its parts are square marks called 'pigeon holes'. Each pigeon hole holds a letter of letters. When the letters are received, they are arranged alphabetically or sequentially.

b. **Folder filing-** There are cardboard covers or thick sheets covered with metal hooks to fasten the papers together. A separate folder is assigned to each customer. All characters associated with that customer are stored in the file's contents. The papers are ordered and filed. The papers lie on top of one another.

c. **Filling with boxes-** The box file, as the name suggests, is made in the form of boxes. The documents are usually placed in folders and then placed in a box file. It helps to keep the papers better as they are safer and collect less dirt. For classification purposes, papers related to various topics may be collated. This method is applicable to traveling agencies where book correspondence is maintained temporarily.

d. **Spike filing-** Includes wire with sharp edges and wood, plastic or round metal at one end is used for filing. It is stored on a table or mounted on the wall after the filling is completed.

e. **Book binds filing-** Under this method, paper or discounts is attached to the book's length. This method is often used to record minutes and save receipts and notes. It avoids the possibility of losing or replacing it incorrectly.

f. **Arch lever fitting-** This system uses sturdy cardboard folders containing solid metal layers. These wires can work with a lever. When the paper is inserted, it is milled through two holes with a milling machine. The excavator is then transferred to the top that opens the edges of the metal or springs. After the paper is inserted into the holes, the lever is pressed down to close the spring. The paper in the file arranges one over the other.

g. Modern Filing Techniques

In addition to traditional filing methods, as mentioned above, you will find some of the most popular modern filing methods nowadays in large and small organizations. Modern filing methods are classified as- (i) Horizontal Filing (ii) Vertical Filing.

a. **Horizontal Filing-** In this system, the documents are stored in file covers or folders one over the other in standard position. The documents are stored chronologically inside the cardboard file cover. Sheets are lined with metallic or metal joints. Files are then stored in cupboards in one convenient place over another. When any paper is required, the correct file is extracted, and after processing it is returned to the same location.

b. **Vertical Filling-** This is a modern form of filling. In this way, the papers are put in files and stored in a straight-standing position. Folders are stored in specially designed cabinets. The front side of the folder is short. The extended back part is used to indicate the file code number. Metal drawer drawings are deep enough to hold vertical folders. In order to separate the wardrobe into simple guide sections are placed in the correct positions. Under this method, it is placed in a separate folder for each customer or subject. Folders can be organized alphabetically, numerically, geographically or intelligently. This system has become very popular in big offices and big business houses.

INDEXING:

Index is a 'point' or 'indicator'. For example, a book index is an index that helps the reader to find pages where various topics have been discussed. Identification is an important issue in filing. It is the process of determining the name, title or other caption where the text is placed. The reference is to the directory. The main purpose of the index is to prepare the location of the required files and documents. Index helps to search the location of any file or text.The objectives of indexing are as follows:

- It helps in searching the location for files and documents.
- It provides quick identification of disconnect.
- It saves time and effort to access records.
- It gives efficiency in the maintenance of records.
- It reduces the cost of running records management.

Types of Indexing-

Indexing can be done in many ways as:

a. **Vertical Card Index**: Each title, document, or customer, is assigned a unique card where relevant information appears. Usually, they are categorized and arranged alphabetically. For example, in the library, two cards are prepared per book- one is arranged on the basis of the author and the other one based on the book.

b. **Strip Index**: It contains a framework in which hard paper sketches are organized in such a way that they can be easily extracted and replaced. Each strap is dedicated to a single item. The frame can be hung on the wall or laid on a table in book form or even arranged in a flexible post that can be turned toward any part of the index.

c. **Fixed Index**: Instead of keeping a separate index, the index may be bound with the relevant document. Such an index usually appears at the end of the standard textbook in which the subject matter is arranged alphabetically and the page numbers are assigned according to each topic or sub-heading.

d. **Loose-Leaf Index**: It is another variation of the index of books. Single sheets are placed in metal pots or screws. Index prepared in these sheets. Whenever a new leaf is added, a book may be opened and a suitable sheet inserted. A bundle containing loose index sheets may be locked so that no pages can be accessed without proper authority.

e. **Wheel or Rotary Index**: Cards are arranged around a tire wheel. One wheel can hold up to 5000 cards. The card can be inserted or removed without interrupting the other cards. Entries can also be made to cards without removing the saddle.

f. **Bound Book Index**: Index prepared in a book that is bound or labeled into paragraphs where the words or texts are inserted.

OFFICE MACHINES AND EQUIPMENT:

Machines and equipment are a significant part to the successful running of any office. We require different types of machines in an office that are essential to perform office tasks quickly and accurately. With rapid technological advancements, there is an increase in the efficiency of office work due to the transfer of high equipped machinery. The use of the office has the following purposes:

- **Increase in accuracy:** One of the purposes of using machines is the accuracy of work especially in every department like attendance monitoring, accounting, sale, purchase, etc.
- **Time-saving:** Machines do more work than they do by hand. They work faster, so there's more time savings.
- **Employee Savings:** few workers can handle large amount of labor and therefore there is a saving of labor.
- **Improving the quality of work:** Work done by machines is usually clean and neat.
- **Ensure better management:** The functioning of the office empowers managers to manage tasks effectively. For example, a biometric thumb impression machine can help manage the attendance of employees.
- **Improving goodwill:** Use of equipment results in better service to customers and the public. This enhances the reputation of the organization.

- **Mitigation of fraud opportunities:** Equipment such as cash register, etc imposes a check on fraud and misuse.

Types of office equipment

Learners must have seen various modern offices. Have you noticed that the offices have turned to automation? Computers can read, store, analyse and interpret information quickly. In the mail room, letters can be opened, sealed, sealed, picked up, weighted and automatically checked with the help of shipping machines. Messages can be sent from one location to another in no time via tele-printer, fax, telephone or internet. Some of the important equipment can be defined as:

- **Computer:** These days, computer is the most commonly used equipment in office. A computer is a machine that can perform various tasks such as calculation, data comparisons, information storage, data analysis and preparation of diagrams and charts.

- **Photocopier Machine:** Photocopier is a machine that makes copies of the paper and other images. It is quick and cheap. Nowadays, photocopiers can print very fast. They even have memory chip which can store the data.
- **Biometric Thumb Impression machine:** In large organizations, arrival and departure of employees is electronically recorded. Thumb impression or swipe card can be used for the same purposes. Employees are given a card with a magnetic strip on it; by swiping them using time recording equipment, arrival and departure times are recorded.
- **Phone/ Intercom:** Nowadays, it's impossible to imagine an office without a phone. It's an easy way to communicate orally widely used in internal and external communications. Cell phones are also very popular nowadays. Compared to fixed phones, mobiles are easier to communicate with at any time. It's also easy to send SMS over the phone. For inter-department communication, an automated communication system i.e., Intercom can be used.
- **Currency counting machine:** This machine is very helpful for departments managing cash. Manual counting of cash may result in mismatch with the cash of balance sheet. It increases accuracy and efficiency.
- **Calculator:** We need concentration during the calculations like addition, subtraction, multiplication, division, percentages, etc. So, calculator can help us for the same and errors can be reduced.
- **Fax:** FAX service enables instant transmission of the facsimile of an entire document. It can send handwritten and printed with pictures, charts and diagrams to different locations within or outside the country. As a result, both the time and labor both is reduced.

- **Projector:** It is a good medium of communication. Through projection, one can communicate the planning and policies between the audiences.

- **Printer and Scanner:** Printer and scanner are essential for office management. We have a variety of printer and scanner like dot matrix printer, inkjet printer, 3D printer, etc. Even now one machine can be used for multiple purposes like 3-in-1 printer i.e. printer, scanner and photocopier.
- **Paper Shredder:** In offices, there are two types of documents. One, those are related to office policies and second, those of no use after some

time i.e. the document with validity. After some time, there is no use to keep such records. So, we can remove such documents. But, if we remove documents as it is, it may disclose the confidentiality of office. So, we should crush the documents first by using the paper shredder machine. This machine cuts the paper in small-small pieces. No one can read the text written over the document.

POINTS TO REMEMBER:

- In current age, mailing services have been changed to electronic mail that can be used to send and receive the text, photos, etc electronically.
- 'Mail' means a written communication via a messenger service or post office. All business concerns send and receive large amounts of letters, notices, circulars, calls, reminder reports, statements, pamphlets, queries, etc.
- The main purpose of the filling process is to ensure proper ordering, proper storage and easy access to records.
- Classification of filing is a process of separating records and documents, organized due to general characteristics prior to completion.
- There are several methods of filing classification, e.g. Serial from 1-100, Serial from A- Z, Geographical, According to the title.
- Indexing is a process of determining the name, title or other caption where the text is placed.

GLOSSARY:

- Bound Book Index: Index prepared in a book that is bound or labelled into paragraphs where the words or texts are inserted.
- Import– The method for bringing data into your program.
- Data Entry– Usually, the process of transferring written or printed data to processable form by keying it character by character.
- Delete– Remove a particular record from a mailing list.

- Edit– Updating a record in a file.
- File– A collection of records on a single storage device.
- Strip Index- It contains a framework in which hard paper sketches are organized in such a way that they can be easily extracted and replaced.

CHAPTER FOUR

INTRODUCTION TO TEXT EDITOR (MS WORD)

INTRODUCTION

MS-Word is a powerful word processor that allows you to create memos, fax cover sheet, web pages, reports, mailing labels, brochures, tables and many other professional and business applications. MS Word provides easy graphics handling, calculation of the data tables, ability to create a mailing list, list sorting and efficient file management.

STARTING MS WORD:

A text editor is any word processing program that you can use to type and edit text. We don't call them text editor for nothing. Word Pad and Notepad for Windows and SimpleText and Text Edit for Mac are common text editors. Larger programs such as Microsoft Word and Word Perfect are also text editors.

Microsoft Word allows you to create professional-quality documents, reports, letters, and résumés. Unlike a plain text editor, Microsoft Word has features including spell check, grammar check, text and font formatting, HTML support, image support, advanced page layout, and more.

Step 1 Click Start Button

Step 2 Click on the 'sub-menu' icon.

Step 3 Click on 'Microsoft Office 2007' from the sub-menu. Step 4 Click on 'Microsoft office word 2007'.

Basics of MS-Word:

- **Tabs:** - Tabs are the predefined functions and features in the word processor, which can be applied for developing certain characteristics on the entered text.
- **Active tab:** - Active tab comprises of seven tabs; home, insert, page layout, references, mailing, review, and view.
- **Ribbon:** - Each tab of the active tab menu has its specific groups of related commands termed as the ribbon.
- **Rulers:** - Rulers help us to control the margins and indentation of pages and paragraphs respectively. They are also used for aligning the images and the text.

- **Document header/footers:** - Headers and footers are being used to display descriptive information such as: page number, document name, date/or time, etc.

- **Document area:** -Document area is a huge blank section of the word processor window which allows the user to enter the contents. This area contains an infinite number of pages which are incremented automatically when the previous page is filled.
- **View buttons:** - View button is a feature that let us see how the document appears or presented.
- **Zoom slider:** - Zoom slider is used to zoom in or zoom out the document pages.

There are many basic operations and functions that we should know before start working in the MS-word, which are listed below:

1. To move the insertion point to the beginning or end of the document

    Press H+> or H+B.

1. To convert a document created in an earlier version of Word

   Click the Microsoft Office Button, and then click Convert.

3. To view multiple pages

   - On the View toolbar, click the Zoom button.
   - In the Zoom dialog box, click the many pages arrow, select the number of pages, and then click OK.

4. To adjust the magnification of a document

   - On the View toolbar, click the Zoom button.
   - In the Zoom dialog box, click on the percentage or type an amount in the Percent box, and then click OK.

5. To display the Document Map

   On the View tab, in the Show/Hide group, select the Document Map checkbox.

6. To display thumbnails of pages

   - On the View tab, in the Show/Hide group, select the Thumbnails checkbox. To display or hide non-printing characters
   - On the Home tab, in the Paragraph group, click the Show/Hide ¶ button.

7. To display a document in a different view

   - On the View tab, in the Document Views group, click the button for the desired view; or
   - Click a view button on the View toolbar at the right end of the status bar.

8. To switch among open documents

   On the View tab, in the Window group, click the Switch Windows button, and then click the name of the document you want to switch to.

9. To view multiple open documents

On the View tab, in the Window group, click the Arrange All button.

10. To open a new document

Click the Microsoft Office Button, click New, and then in the New Document window, double-click Blank document.

11. To save a document for the first time

- On the Quick Access Toolbar, click the Save button; or click the Microsoft Office Button, and then click Save As.
- If Browse Folders is shown in the lower-left corner of the Save As dialog box, click it, and then navigate to the location where you want to save the file.
- In the File name box, type a name for the document, and then click Save.

12. To create a new folder while saving a document

- Click the Microsoft Office Button, and then click Save As.
- In the Save As dialog box, navigate to the folder where you want to create the new folder.
- On the dialog box's toolbar, click the New Folder button
- Type the name of the new folder, press F, and then click Open.
- In the File name box, type a name for the document, and then click Save.

13. To preview how a document will look when printed

Click the Microsoft Office Button, point to print, and then click Print Preview.

14. To print a document with the default settings

Click the Microsoft Office Button, point to print, and then click Quick Print.

15. To print a document with custom settings

- Click the Microsoft Office Button, and then click Print.
- In the Print dialog box, modify the settings as needed, and then click OK

16. To select text

- Word: Double-click the word.
- Sentence: Click in the sentence while holding down the H key.
- Paragraph: Triple-click in the paragraph, or double-click in the selection area to the left of the paragraph.
- Block: Click to the left of the first word, hold down the G key, and then click immediately to the right of the last word or punctuation mark.
- Line: Click in the selection area to the left of the line.
- Document: Triple-click in the selection area. To delete text
- Select the text, and then press A or Z.

17. To undo an action

On the Quick Access Toolbar, click the Undo button.

18. To move text by dragging

- Select the text, and then point to the selection.
- Hold down the mouse button, drag the text to its new location, and then release the mouse button.

19. To save text as a building block

- Select the text. Then on the Insert tab, in the Text group, click the Quick Parts button and then click Save Selection to Quick Part Gallery.

- In the Create New Building Block dialog box, type a name for the building block, make any necessary changes to the settings, and then click OK.

20. To insert a building block in a document

Click where you want to insert the building block. Then either type the name of the building block, and press #; or on the Insert tab, in the Text group, click the Quick Parts button, and select the building block from the Quick Part gallery.

21. To insert the date and time

   - Click where you want the date or time to appear, and then on the Insert tab, in the Text group, click the Date & Time button.
   - In the Date and Time dialog box, under Available formats, click the format you want, and then click OK.

22. To use the Thesaurus

   - Double-click the word you want to replace, and then on the Review tab, in the Proofing group, click the Thesaurus button.
   - In the Research task pane, point to the word you want to insert in place of the selected word, click the arrow that appears, and then click Insert.

23. To research information

   - On the Review tab, in the Proofing group, click Research.
   - In the Research task pane, in the Search for box, type the research topic.
   - Click the arrow of the box below the Search for box, click the resource you want to use, and then in the results list, click a source to view its information.

24. To translate a word or phrase into another language

   - Select the word or phrase, and then on the Review tab, in the Proofing group, click the Translate button.
   - In the Translation area of the Research task pane, select the desired languages in the form and to boxes to display the translation.

25. To display a document in Outline view

   On the View toolbar, click the Outline button.

26. To display specific heading levels in Outline view

On the Outlining tab, in the Outline Tools group, click the Show Level arrow, and in the list, click a heading level.

27. To collapse or expand heading levels in Outline view

Click anywhere in the heading to be collapsed or expanded. Then on the Outlining tab, in the Outline Tools group, click the Collapse or Expand button.

28. To demote or promote headings in Outline view

Click the heading to be demoted or promoted. Then on the Outlining tab, in the Outline Tools group, click the Demote or Promote button.

29. To move content in Outline view

Collapse the heading whose text you want to move. Then on the Outlining tab, in the Outline Tools group, click the Move Up or Move Down button.

30. To find text

- On the Home tab, in the Editing group, click the Find button.
- On the Find tab of the Find and Replace dialog box, specify the text you want to find, and then click Find Next.

31. To replace text

- On the Home tab, in the Editing group, click the Replace button.
- On the Replace tab of the Find and Replace dialog box, specify the text you want to find and the text you want to replace it with, and then click Find Next.
- Click Replace to replace the first instance of the text, Replace All to replace all instances, or Find Next to leave that instance unchanged and move to the next one.

32. To check spelling and grammar

- On the Review tab, in the Proofing group, click the Spelling & Grammar button.
- In the Spelling and Grammar dialog box, click the appropriate buttons to correct the errors Word finds or to add words to the custom dictionary or AutoCorrect list.
- Click OK when Word reaches the end of the Spelling and Grammar check, and then click Close.

33. To remove personal information from a document

- Click the Microsoft Office Button, point to Prepare, and then click Inspect Document.
- In the Document Inspector dialog box, select the items you want to be checked, and then click Inspect.
- In the Document Inspector summary, click the Remove All button to the right of any items you want to be removed, and then close the Document Inspector dialog box.

34. To mark a document as final

- Click the Microsoft Office Button, point to Prepare, and then click Mark as Final.

- Click OK in the message box, click Save, and then click OK in the finalization message.

35. Changing the Look of: Click the paragraph or select the text to which you want to apply a style. Then on the Home tab in the Styles group, click the thumbnail of the style you want to apply in the Quick Styles gallery.

<u>WORKING WITH DOCUMENT:</u>

Entering and saving text in a document-

Entering and saving of the data in MS-word is very easy. A blinking cursor appears in the text area which decides the position of the text to be entered. We can enter the contents in the text area with not only various formats of writing but also different size, shapes, and colors. We can also apply certain features like bold, italic, and underline and can arrange the position of the contents through various aligning icons. We can save the entered content by shortcut key (CTRL+S) OR can go through various steps given below:

Step 1:Click on the 'office button' present at the top left corner of the screen.

Step2: Now, click on the 'save' option from the menu. Or Click on the 'save as' option to provide a custom name to your document.

Closing the MS Word-

If you want to close the MS-Word window so, you just have to click on the 'X' icon present on the right top corner of the window. As you click on the 'X' icon, a small dialog box appears which ask you for saving the document. If you want to save the document just click on the 'yes' option, that will close the window after saving your document, else click on the 'no' option that will close the window without saving your document.

Opening an existing document-

We can open our previously saved documents by just clicking on the office button present at the top left part of the MS-Word window. As we click on the 'open' option from the menu a document window appears which contain all the previously saved documents. All we have to do is select the desired document from the list and click on the 'Open'.

Copy and Cut (Move)-

Copy and the cut commands are used for transferring data from one place to another within the page or between the different pages of multiple documents. The copy command transfers the replica of the original data while the cut command transfers the original data to another place. We can perform both the operations by selecting the 'copy' or 'cut' options from the dialog box that appears on right-clicking the mouse after selecting the desired data.

After clicking on any one of the two options, just position the mouse on the area you want the data to appear and select the 'paste' command by right-clicking on the mouse.

WORKING WITH SYMBOLS, GRAPHICS, AND EQUATIONS:

We have several disciplines, different areas and fields where documentation work is highly preferred. A certain number of equations, pie-charts, graphs, and other quantitative properties are required in a document. As a result, we have to perform many changes, including several equations and others formatting to our documents. There are some of the working criteria in the MS-Word which are highly used.

1. To insert a picture

- Click where you want to insert the picture. Then on the Insert tab in the Illustrations group, click the Picture button.
- Navigate to the folder where the picture is stored, and then double-click the picture to insert it.

2. To adjust the size of an object

Click the object. Then point to one of the handles surrounding the object, and when the pointer becomes a two-headed arrow, drag until the picture is the size you want.

3. To insert clip art

- Click where you want to insert the clip art. Then on the Insert tab, in the Illustrations group, click the Clip Art button
- In the Clip Art task pane, in the Search for box, type a word describing what you are looking for, and then click Go.
- In the task pane, click a clip art image to insert it in the document, and then close the task pane.

4. To move an object

Click the object to select it. Then point to the object and when the pointer changes to a four-headed arrow, drag the object to the new position.

5. To quickly copy an object

Click the object, hold down the H key, and then drag a copy of the object to its new location, releasing first the mouse button and then the F key.

6. To insert a WordArt object

- Click where you want to insert the WordArt. Then on the Insert tab, in the Text group, click the WordArt button.
- In the WordArt gallery, click the style you want.
- In the Edit WordArt Text dialog box, type your text.
- Set the size and other attributes of the text, and then click OK.

7. To apply a drop cap

Click in the paragraph. Then on the Insert tab, in the Text group, click the Drop Cap button, and click the style you want.

8. To draw a shape

- On the Insert tab, in the Illustrations group, click the Shapes button, and then click the shape you want.
- Point where you want the shape to appear, and then drag to draw the shape.

9. To group draw objects

- Hold down the H key, and click each object you want to group.
- On the Format contextual tab in the Arrange group, click the Group button, and then click Group.

10. To change the text wrapping of a picture

Select the picture. Then on the Format contextual tab, in the Arrange group, click the Text Wrapping button, and click the wrapping style and attributes you want.

11. To change the position of a picture

Select the picture. Then point to the picture and when the pointer changes to a four- headed arrow, drags the picture to its new location. Or
Select the picture. Then on the Format contextual tab in the Arrange group, click the Picture button, and click More Layout Options
In the Advanced Layout dialog box, on the Picture Position tab, set the position options you want, and then click OK.

12. To insert a symbol

- Click where you want to insert the symbol. Then on the Insert tab, in the Symbols group, click the Symbol button, and click More Symbols.
- In the Symbols dialog box, on the Symbols tab, select the font you want
- Scroll through the list of symbols until you find the symbol you want, double-click it, and then click Close.

13. To insert an equation

- Click where you want to insert the equation. Then on the Insert tab in the Symbols group, click the Equation button.
- Type your equation in the equation box that appears in the document.

WORKING WITH DIAGRAMS AND CHARTS:

1. To insert a diagram

- Click where you want to insert the diagram. Then on the Insert tab in the Illustrations group, click the SmartArt button.
- In the Choose a SmartArt Graphic dialog box, click the diagram layout you want, and then click OK.

2. To add text to a diagram

Click the placeholder text in the 'Type your text here' pane or in the diagram shape, and then type your text.

3. To resize a diagram

Drag a sizing handle around the diagram frame and then drag the handle to increase or decrease the size of the diagram.

4. To add a shape to a diagram

Click the diagram shape above or below which you want the new shape to appear. Then on the Design contextual tab in the Create Graphic group, click the Add Shape arrow. And in the list, click Add Shape After, Add Shape Before, Add Shape Above, or Add Shape Below.

5. To change the diagram layout

Click a blank area in the diagram's frame. Then, on the Design contextual tab in the Layouts group, click the more button. And in the gallery, click the layout you want.

6. To move a diagram

Point to the diagram's frame (not one of the handles), and when the pointer changes to a four-headed arrow, drag the diagram to its new location.

7. To change the style of a diagram

Click a blank area inside the diagram's frame. Then on the Design tab, in the SmartArt Styles group, click the more button. In the gallery, click the style you want.

8. To insert a chart

*   On the Insert tab in the Illustrations group, click Chart.

- In the Insert Chart dialog box, click the category of chart you want, click the style you want, and then click OK.

9. To enter data in a new chart

In the Excel worksheet, replace the sample data by clicking a cell, and then type your own data.

10. To fit a column to its longest entry

Point to the border between two column headings and when the pointer changes to a double-headed arrow, double-click.

11. To edit the data in a selected chart

- On the Design tab, in the Data group, click the Edit Data button.
- In the Excel worksheet, click the cell you want to edit, type the new data, and then press F.

12. To change the type of a selected chart

- On the Design tab in the Type group, click the Change Chart Type button.
- In the Change Chart Type dialog box, click the chart type you want, and then click OK.

13. To change the style of a selected chart

On the Design tab, in the Chart Styles group, click the more button, and in the Chart Styles gallery, click the style you want.

14. To turn a chart's gridlines on and off

On the Layout contextual tab in the Axes group, click the Gridlines button. Point to the Primary Horizontal Gridlines or Primary Vertical Gridlines, and click the option you want.

<u>Working with professional documents:</u>
(E.g. Reports/ Thesis/ Proposal, etc.)

1. To delete a building block

- In the Text group, click Quick Parts, and then click Building Blocks Organizer.
- In the Building blocks list, select the building block you want to delete, and then click Delete.

2. To create a table of contents based on headings

- Position the insertion point; you want to insert the table of contents. Then, on the References tab, in the Table of Contents group, click the Table of Contents button.

- In the Table of Contents gallery, click the table of contents style you want.

3. To update a table of contents

- Click in the table of contents. Then on the References tab, in the Table of Contents group, click the Update Table button.
- In the Update Table of Contents dialog box, click Update page numbers only or Update entire table, and then click OK.

4. To insert an index entry

- Select the word you want to mark. Then, on the References tab in the Index group, click the Mark Entry button.
- In the Mark Index Entry dialog box, click Mark.

5. To create an index

- Click where you want to insert the index. Then, on the Home tab in the Paragraph group, click the Show/Hide button to turn off the display of non-printing characters
- On the References tab in the Index group, click Insert Index. In the Index dialog box, click the Formats arrow, click an index format, select any other options you want, and then click OK.

6. To insert a bookmark

- Select the text or item that you want to bookmark. Then, on the Insert tab in the Links group, click Bookmark.
- In the Bookmark dialog box, in the Bookmark name box, type the bookmark name (with no spaces) or select one from the list of bookmarks, and then click Add.

7. To insert a cross-reference

- Click where you want to insert the cross-reference. Then type the introductory text for the cross reference; for example, for more information, see.
- On the Insert tab, in the Links group, click the Cross-reference button.
- In the Cross-reference dialog box, click the Reference type arrow, and then click the type of reference you want.
- Click the Insert reference to arrow, and then click the type of item you are referencing, if necessary.
- In the 'For which' box, click the item you are referencing to, click Insert, and then click Close.

Finding a Particular Pattern-

A pattern is a simple, repeating overlay of a one-color design over a background of another color. We can apply the pattern on different objects and on various sections and part of the documents with the help of given steps:

Step 1. Right-click the shape and choose Format Shape. The Format Shape dialog box opens.

Step 2. Click the Fill tab.

Step 3. Click the Pattern Fill option button. The controls change to show pattern options.

Step 4. Click the desired pattern.

Step 5. Open the Foreground Color menu and select the foreground color. As with other color selectors, you can select a theme color, a tint or shade, or a standard color.

Step 6. Open the Background Color menu and select the background color.

Step 7. Click Close to close the dialog box.

Inserting objects into a document-

Depending on the version of Word or Outlook you're using, you can insert a variety of objects (such as PDF files, Excel charts or worksheets, or PowerPoint presentations) into a Word document or an email message by linking or embedding them.

1. To insert an object

- Click Object on the Insert tab.
- Insert a new object

2. To create a new file that is inserted into your Word document or email message

In the Object dialog box, click the Create New tab, and then select an option from the Object type list.

The default program for that file type opens, where you can enter any text or data you want. When you close the program, any added content or changes appear in your Word document or email message.

If you want the new file to appear as a clickable icon, rather than the first page of your new file, select Display as icon. If this check box is selected, you can choose a different icon by clicking Change Icon.

Tips:

- The information in the Result section changes based on the selected object type and whether Display as icon is selected. Use this information to help you determine what you want to insert and how you want it to appear.
- To edit the information in your inserted object, double-click the object.

3. Link or embed an existing file

To link or embed an object that's already been created:

- In the Object dialog box, select the Create from File tab, and then click Browse to find the file you want to insert.

- To link to the source file, rather than embedding it into your Word document or email message, select Link to file.
- If you want the inserted file to appear as a clickable icon, rather than the first page of the file, select Display as icon. If this check box is selected, you can choose a different icon by clicking Change Icon.

Tip: The information in the Result section changes based on whether Link to file and Display as icon are selected. Use this information to help you determine what you want to insert and how you want it to appear.

Embedded objects vs. linked objects

Embedded objects become part of the Word file or email message and, after they are inserted, they are no longer connected to any source file.

Linked objects can be updated if the source file is modified. Linked data is stored in the source file. The Word file or email message (the destination file) stores only the location of the source file, and it displays a representation of the linked data. Use linked objects if the file size is a consideration.

POINTS TO REMEMBER:

- Microsoft Word is a word processing program, designed to help you create professional-quality documents.
- With the finest document formatting tools, word helps you organize and write your documents more efficiently.
- Word also includes powerful editing and revising tools so that you can collaborate with others easily.
- We have learnt how to create our own documents, open existing documents and finally save them before closing.

GLOSSARY:

- **Title Bar:** It displays the document name followed by a program name.

- **Menu Bar:** It contains a list of options to manage and customize documents.
- **Standard Toolbar:** It contains shortcut buttons for the most popular commands.
- **Formatting Toolbar:** It contains buttons used for formatting.
- **Ruler:** Ruler is used to set margins, indents, and tabs.
- **Status Bar:** It displays the position of the insertion point and working mode buttons.
- **Scroll Bars:** These are used to view parts of the document.

CHAPTER FIVE

INTRODUCTION TO SPREADSHEET (MS EXCEL)

INTRODUCTION

MS-EXCEL is a very powerful and easy-to-use spreadsheet package. It is a member- application included in the MS Office suite. It works very well with numbers and their complex calculations. There are numbers of spreadsheet programs, but from all of them, Excel is most widely used. The best part about Excel is that it's applicable to many business tasks, including finance, data management, forecasting statistics, analysis, inventory, billing, and business intelligence.

STARTING MS EXCEL

Microsoft Excel is a spreadsheet program used to record and analyse numerical data. Spreadsheets were originally developed for book keeping; however, they are also useful for data manipulation and producing graphs. Spreadsheet as a collection of columns and rows form a table. Alphabetical letters are usually assigned to columns and numbers are usually assigned to rows. The point where a column and a row meet is called a cell. The address of a cell is given by the letter representing the column and the number representing a row.

The MS Excel interface-

Starting MS Excel- To start-up the MS Excel follow the following steps-
Step 1- Open the Windows Start menu

Step 2- Choose All Programs then Microsoft Office followed by Microsoft Office Excel 2013

Step 3-You can create a shortcut to this software by dragging Microsoft Excel from this menu onto the Desktop using the right mouse button – select Create shortcut here from the popup menu.

The MS Excel interface basic tools and commands-

1. **Active Cell-**

A cell in excel spreadsheet which is currently selected by clicking on it will be highlighted by a rectangular box.

1. Column-

A column is a vertical set of cells in a spreadsheet. Every column has its own alphabet for identity. You can select a column clicking on its header.

3. Row-

A row is a horizontal set of cells. Every row has its own number for identity. You can select a row clicking on the row number marked on the left side of the window.

4. Fill Handle-

It's a small dot present on the lower right corner of the active cell. It used to fill numeric values, text series, insert ranges, insert serial numbers, etc.

5. Address Bar-

The address bar is the small input bar at the left side of the window. It shows the address of the active cell. We can select more than one cell, and then it will show the address of the first cell in the range.

6. Formula Bar-

The formula bar is an input bar, below the ribbon. It is used to enter a formula in a cell.

7. Title Bar-

The title bar lies in the middle and at the top of the window. It shows the program and sheet titles.

8. File Menu-

The file menu is a simple menu like in all other applications. It contains options like (Save, Save As, Open, New, Print, Excel Options, Share, etc).

9. Quick Access Toolbar-

This you will find just above the file menu and its purpose is to provide a convenient resting place for the Excel's most frequently used commands. You can customize this toolbar based on your comfort.

10. Ribbon Tab-

Starting from the Microsoft Excel 2007, all the options menus are replaced with the ribbons. The ribbon contains commands organized in three components: Tabs, Groups, and Commands

11. Worksheet Tab-

This tab shows all the worksheets present in the workbook. By default you will see, three worksheets in your new workbook with a name of Sheet1, Sheet2, and Sheet3 respectively.

12. Status Bar-

This displays sheet information as well as the insertion point location. From left to right this bar can contain the total number of pages and words in the document, language, etc.

BASIC FUNCTIONALITIES OF MS EXCEL:

Exiting MS EXCEL-

When you are ready to quit Excel, you have different choices for exit the program:

- Select File -> Exit.
- Press Alt+F4.
- Click the Close button in the upper- right corner of the Excel 2013 Program window.

Working with Workbook-

Excel files are called workbooks. In Microsoft Excel, a workbook is a collection of one or more spreadsheets, also called worksheet, in a single file. A workbook is another word for Excel File. When we start Excel, click blank workbook to create an Excel workbook from the scratch.

Creating a new Workbook-

Whenever you start a new project in excel, you will need to create a new workbook, execute the following steps.

Step 1 On the file tab, Backstage view will appear Step 2 Select new, and then click the blank workbook Step 3 A new blank workbook will appear.

Working with cells-

The interaction of rows and columns is called a cell. Cell is identified with a combination of the column header and row number.

Setting Font-

You can assign any of the fonts that are installed for your printer to cells in a worksheet. You can set the font of the selected text from Home>>Font group>> select the font. Setting font from format cell dialogue-

Step 1 Right click on cell >> Format cells >> Font Tab Step 2 Press Ctrl + 1 or Shift + Ctrl + F

Text Formatting-

Various options available in "Home Tab" of ribbon as below:

- Bold: It makes text highlighted by choosing Home>> Font Group>> Click B or Press Ctrl + B
- Italic: It makes text italic by choosing Home>> Font group>> Click I or Press Ctrl + I
- Underline: It makes text to be underlined by choosing Home>> Font group>> Click U or Press Ctrl + U
- Double Underline: It makes text double underline by choosing Home>> Font group>> Click the arrow near U >> Select double underline
- Strike-through: It makes strikes the text in the center vertically.
- Super Script: It makes the character (such as a number or letter) appear slightly above the normal line of type usually smaller than the rest of the text.
- Sub Script: It makes the character appear slightly below the normal line of type.

Change Alignment-

You can change horizontal and vertical alignment of the cell. By default, Excel aligns numbers to the right and text to the left. Click on the available option in the Alignment group in Home Tab to change alignment. Right click on the cell and select format cell. In format cells dialogue select Alignment Tab and select the available options from the vertical alignment and horizontal alignment options.

Horizontal Alignment: You can set horizontal alignment to Left, Centre, Right, etc. Left: Aligns the cell contents to the left side of the cell

Centre: Centres the cell contents in the cell Right: Aligns the cell contents to the right side of the cell Justify: Justify the text to the left and right of the cell.

Vertical Alignment: You can set vertical alignment to Top, Middle, Bottom, etc. Top: Aligns the cell contents to the top of the cell.

Centre: Centres the cell contents vertically in the cell. Bottom: Aligns the cell contents to the bottom of the cell.

Merging of Cells-

MS Excel enables you to merge two or more cells. When you merge cells, you don't combine

the contents of cells. You combine a group of cells into a single cell that occupies the same space. Select Merge and Centre control on the Ribbon is simpler. To merge cells, select the cells that you want to merge and then click the Merge and Centre button. Select alignment tab of the format cells dialogue box to merge cells. The Home>> Alignment Group>> Merge and Centre control contains a drop-down list with these additional options:

Merge Across: When a multi row range is selected, this command creates multiple merged cells- one for each row.

Merge Cells: Merges the selected cells without applying the centre attribute Unmerge Cells: Unmerges the selected cells.

Wrap Text and Shrink to Fit-

If you have text too wide to fit the column width but don't want that text to spill over into adjacent cells, you can use either the wrap Text option or the Shrink to fit option to be accommodating the text.

INSERTING, DELETING ROWS AND COLUMNS:

Inserting Rows and Columns

To insert a row or column into a Microsoft Excel worksheet:

Step 1 Select a cell in your worksheet, you would like the new row or column to be inserted. To select multiple rows or columns simply select multiple cells.

[1] New rows are inserted above the selected cell.

[2] New columns are inserted above the selected cell.

Step 2 On the Home tab in the cells group, click the Insert command.

Step 3 Select Insert Sheet Rows or Insert Sheet Columns:

Deleting Rows and Columns

To delete a row or column into a Microsoft Excel worksheet:

Step 1 Select a cell in your worksheet in the new row or column you wish to delete. To delete multiple rows or columns, simply select multiple cells.

Step 2 On the Home tab in the cells group, click the Delete command.

Step 3 Select Delete Sheet Rows or Delete Sheet Columns.

SAVING AND CLOSING WORKBOOK:

Saving a Workbook-

It's important to save your workbook whenever you start a new project or make changes to an existing one. Execute the following steps.

Step 1 Locate and select the save command on the Quick Access toolbar.

Step 2 If you are saving file for the first time, the Save As pane will appear in the backstage view.

Step 3 You will then need to select where to save the file and give it a file name. To save the workbook to your computer, select computer, then click OneDrive to save the file to your OneDrive.

Step 4 The Save As dialog box will appear. Select the location where you want to save the workbook.

Step 5 Enter a file name for the workbook, then click save.

Step 6 The workbook will be saved. You can click save command again to save your changes as you modify the workbook.

You can also access the save command by pressing Ctrl + S on your keyboard.

Closing a Workbook-

To close a workbook, follow below given steps-

Step 1 Click on the File tab in the main menu.

Step 2 Click on close.

If the file gets saved then, it will get closed; otherwise, you will get a message "want to save changes in xxxx.xls".

If you want to save changes just click on save.

POINTS TO REMEMBER:

- MS Excel is a very powerful and easy to use spreadsheet packages, perhaps the most commonly used these days. It is a member application included in the MS Office suite. It works very well with numbers and their complex calculations.

- Spreadsheets were originally developed for bookkeeping; however, they are also useful for data manipulation and producing for graphs. Spreadsheet as a collection of columns and rows form a table. Excel can sort and select data for a large amount of data or more complex task.

GLOSSARY:

- Cell: A cell is a box at the intersection of a row and column in a worksheet where data is stored.
- Column: Columns are a combination of all the vertical cells joined together in a single vertical line.
- Row: Rows are a combination of all the horizontal cells joined together in a single horizontal line.
- Workbook: It is a group of worksheets, which can be stored as a unit. A workbook is stored on the disk in the form of a file with extension .xls.
- Worksheet: It is the working area of MS-EXCEL. Each worksheet of a single workbook has its own identity and is separate from other worksheets.
- Workspace: It is the working area of MS-Excel where workbooks, worksheets and other related objects may be opened and manipulated.

CHAPTER SIX

INTRODUCTION TO PRESENTATION (MS POWER POINT)

INTRODUCTION

PowerPoint is similar to a word processor such as Word, except that it specializes in creating presentations rather than documents. A presentation is like those Kodak Carousel slide trays that your grandpa filled up with 35mm slides of the time he took the family to the Grand Canyon in 1965. The main difference is that with Microsoft PowerPoint 2019, you don't have to worry about dumping all the slides out of the tray and figuring out how to get them back into the right order.

Word documents consist of one or more pages, and PowerPoint presentations consist of one or more slides. Each slide can contain text, graphics, animations, videos, and other information. You can easily rearrange the slides in a presentation, delete slides that you don't need, add new slides, or modify the contents of existing slides.

STARTING MS POWER POINT:

MS PowerPoint interface-
You can start Microsoft PowerPoint in just a few simple steps.

Step 1 Click on the PowerPoint icon in the Taskbar. If you do not see the icon, go to the Start button, right-click, and choose Search. Type "PowerPoint" in the search field, and when PowerPoint appears, double-click it. (Windows 7: Go to the Start button, then All Programs and choose PowerPoint.)

Step 2 PowerPoint will open, prompting you to select a theme. Click on the Blank Presentation.

The MS PowerPoint interface quick explanation-

- **Quick Access**- This button positions top left portion, this toolbar is customizable; you can move this in two possible locations. This toolbar consists of a set of commands that it is independent on the tab of the ribbon currently displayed and you can add commands in this button.
- **Title Bar**- Position at the top of the user interface, where the file name will see here after saving a file, as a default once you open your MS-Office 2010 you will see it as Presentation1Microsoft PowerPoint.
- **Control Tool Box**- Located right top of the user interface, where you can close, restore and maximize, and minimize the windows program.
- **Tab Menu or a tab of the ribbon**- Position below of the title bar, this relates to the type of activity, such as to relate a ribbon menu name, like once you click the home it will open as home ribbon menu. The tab menus are FILE, HOME, INSERT, DESIGN, TRANSITIONS, ANIMATIONS, SLIDE SHOW, REVIEW, and VIEW.
- **Ribbon Menu**- Position under of the tab menus, if you need to see it or control it, hold CTRL key and press F1. This menu contains all the commands and other menu items that you can help to find the command easily to finish your work.
- **Slide Sorter**- Position left side of your user interface, all the slides will arrange in vertical order from the top as first slides down to your last slides. You can drag to rearrange the slides, delete, and give other command once you right click your mouse.
- **Slide Template**- This part is position at the centre of your user interface, this is the biggest part where you can start and put your design in Presentation, animation, effects and more.
- **Animation Pane**- It is a part and command of ANIMATION PANE, once you click this button, it will open in the right-side portion of your user interface. This pane or panel will display the animation functions you use in your slide template. Also, you can rearrange the animation and

effects according to your own design.

- **Zoom In and Out Sliding Bar**- This part position right side down and above of the taskbar. This is used to enlarge and decrease the view of your slide template at the center.
- **Add Note or Notes Pane**- This pane or panel position at the bottom of your user interface. You can type notes that you can accompany a slide. You can print these notes as notes pages or display it when you save a presentation as a web page.
- **Status Bar**- This part position below of the user interface and left side of the zoom in/out sliding bar and view buttons of the slide show. This is only to notify what slide number you use in your application.

Exiting MS PowerPoint-

After you have created a new presentation file and spent some time working on it, you will want to save it every so often so that when your system crashes, you can recover your work. And if you are like most folks, you'll also want to save and close your presentation each time you wrap up a work session.

Saving and closing a PowerPoint presentation are both straightforward tasks. If you are familiar with any other Windows programs, then you will recognize most of the steps. To save a newly created presentation:

Step 1 Select Office button> Save. The Save As dialog box appears.

Most of the time, when you're ready to save your presentation, you'll choose the .pptx file type or .ppt (the old, pre-2007 PowerPoint format). But you have got about a dozen choices, including the template (.potx) and show (.ppsx) formats.

You can press Ctrl+S or click the Save button (the little diskette icon) that appears in the Quick Access toolbar.

Step 2 Click the Save in the drop-down box to choose a directory to store your file in. In the File name field, type a new name for your file.

Step 3 Click the Save as Type drop-down box to select a file format. Most of the time, you will choose the .pptx format and click Save. The Save As dialog box disappears and PowerPoint saves the file in the format you specified.

Step 4 To close a presentation, simply select Office Close. When you do, PowerPoint closes your presentation with no fanfare. If you have never saved this particular file, however, a dialog box pops up asking you if you want to save the changes you made. Click Yes to display the Save As dialog box and proceed as described above.

DIFFERENT TYPES OF VIEWS:

PowerPoint supports multiple views to allow users to gain the maximum from the features available in the program. Each view supports a different set of functions and is designed accordingly. PowerPoint views can be accessed from two locations.

1. Views can be accessed quickly from the bottom bar just to the left of the zoom settings.
2. Views can also be accessed from the Presentation Views section in the View ribbon Here is a short description of the various views and their features.

a. **Normal View**- This is the default view in PowerPoint, and this is primarily used to create and edit slides. You can create/ delete/ edit/ rearrange slides, add/ remove/

modify content and manipulate sections from this view.

a. **Slide Sorter View**- This view is primarily used to sort slides and rearrange them. This view is also ideal for adding or removing sections as it presents the slides in a more

compact manner making it easier to rearrange them.

c. **Reading View**- This view is new to PowerPoint 2010, and it was created mainly to review the slideshow without losing access to rest of the Windows applications. Typically, when you run the slideshow, the presentation takes up the entire screen so other applications cannot be accessed from the taskbar. In the reading view, the taskbar is still available while viewing the slideshow which is convenient. You cannot make any modifications when on this view.

Slides Show- This is the traditional slideshow view available in all the earlier versions of PowerPoint. This view is used to run the slideshow during presentation.

CREATING PRESENTATION:

In Microsoft PowerPoint, a presentation is made up of multiple slides. There are several ways to create or add a slide in a PowerPoint presentation. After adding slides, you can move the slides around, and you can delete slides.

1. Working with Slides

   Insert new slide-
   To insert a new slide into a presentation, follow the steps below.

- In the slide preview pane on the left, left-click with your mouse in-between two slides where you want to insert a slide.
- In the PowerPoint ribbon, on the Home or Insert tab, click the New Slide option.
- In the drop-down menu that opens, select the type of slide to insert. The new slide will be inserted into the presentation where you clicked in step 1 above.

   Copy and paste an existing slide-
   To add a copy of an existing slide to a presentation, follow the steps below.

- In the slide preview pane on the left, find the existing slide you want to copy.
- Using your mouse, right-click on that slide and select Copy in the pop-up menu.
- Determine where you want to add the copied slide. Right-click on the slide above, you want to paste the copied slide.
- In the pop-up menu that appears, in the Paste Options section, click the middle paste option icon to paste the slide. The middle paste option will paste the slide using the same formatting as the slide you copied.

   Insert slide from another presentation-
   To add a slide from another presentation, follow the steps below.

- In the slide preview pane on the left, left-click with your mouse in-between two slides where you want to insert a slide.
- In the PowerPoint ribbon, on the Home or Insert tab, click the New Slide option.
- In the drop-down menu that opens, click the Reuse Slides option at the bottom.
- In the Reuse Slides pane that opens on the right, click the Browse button and select Browse File.
- Find the PowerPoint presentation file that contains the slide you want to add to the currently open presentation and click the Open button.
- A preview of the slides is displayed below the Browse option. Left-click on the slide you want to insert into the currently open presentation. A new slide will be inserted, with text from the selected slide included in the new slide.
- To also apply the formatting of the selected slide to the newly inserted slide, right-click on the selected slide and select Apply Theme to Selected Slides.

Move a slide-

To move a slide to another location in a PowerPoint presentation, follow the steps below.

- Open the PowerPoint presentation.
- In the left preview pane, find the slide you want to move.
- Press and hold the left mouse button on the slide, then drag the slide up or down to where you want to move it.
- Release the left mouse button when you have dragged the slide to its new location.

Delete a slide-

To delete a slide in a PowerPoint presentation, follow the steps below.

- Open the PowerPoint presentation.
- In the left preview pane, click on the slide you want to delete.
- Press the delete key to delete the slide.

2. Working with new presentation-

- Create presentations from scratch or a template.
- Add text, images, art, and videos.
- Select a professional design with a PowerPoint Designer.
- Add transitions, animations, and motion.
- Save to OneDrive to get your presentations from your computer, tablet, or phone.
- Share and work with others wherever they are.

Create a Presentation-

- Select Blank Presentation to create a presentation from scratch.
- Select one of the templates.
- Select Take a Tour, and then select Create, to see tips for using PowerPoint.

Adding slide-

- Select the slide you want your new slide to follow.
- Select Home > New Slide.

- Select Layout and then type what you want from the drop-down.

Add text and format text-

- Place the cursor where you want, and type.
- Select the text, and then select an option on the Home tab: Font, Font size, Bold, Italic, Underline, etc.

- To create bulleted or numbered lists, select the text, and then select Bullets or Numbering.

Adding a picture, shape, or chart-

- Select Insert tab, then to add a picture- Select Picture or Browse for the picture you want and select Insert.
- To add a shape, art, or chart- Select Shapes, Icons, SmartArt, or Chart

DESIGN TEMPLATES:

PowerPoint offers design templates to make it easy to create an attractive presentation. These templates come in a variety of colors and styles. You can apply a design to existing slides or begin a new presentation with a template. To begin a new presentation with a design template:

- In the task pane under New, click From Design Template.
- A list of templates appears.
- Move your mouse pointer through the different designs or use the scroll bar.
- Click the down-pointing arrow in the gray box next to the template you like.
- Choose Apply to All Slides.

Adding a design to an existing presentation-

Do you have an existing presentation you want to add a design to? PowerPoint makes it easy to enhance existing slides with a design template. To apply a design to an existing presentation:

- In the task pane, under Open a presentation, click the presentation you want.
- Click the down-pointing arrow in the New Presentation pane and choose Slide Design - Design Templates.
- A list of templates appears.
- Move your mouse pointer through the different designs or use the scroll bar.
- Click the down-pointing arrow in the gray box next to the template you like.
- Choose Apply to All Slides.

Applying a design template to selected slides-

As you are working on your presentation, you can choose Apply to Selected Slides if you want one or more slides to have a different look.

APPLYING CUSTOM ANIMATION AND SLIDE TRANSITION:

Custom Animation-

We can apply the custom animation with the certain steps given below-

- Select the text or object.
- Select the Animation tab.
- In Animation group, click the Custom Animation.
- Custom Animation task pane appears on the right.
- Click the Add Effect. It will display four options that are further divided into different options.
- Select the desired effect.

Slide Transition-

Transition effects appear when one slide changes into next slide in a slide show.

- Select the slide to which you want to apply the effect.
- Select the Animation tab.
- In Transition to This Slide group, you will see the transition effects.
- Click the drop-down arrow to see the menu of transition effects.
- Select the desired transition effect.
- Click Apply to All to apply the effect to all slides.

MISCELLANEOUS POINTS- PRESENTATION:

Saving a presentation-

PowerPoint offers two ways to save a file: Save and Save As. These options work in similar ways, with a few important differences.

- Save: When you create or edit a presentation, you'll use the Save command to save your changes. You'll use this command most of the time. When you save a file, you'll only need to choose a file name and location the first time. After that, you can just click the Save command to save it with the same name and location.
- Save As: You'll use this command to create a copy of a presentation while keeping the original. When you use Save As, you'll need to choose a different name and/or location for the copied version.

Note- Using "Save As" to make a copy-

If you want to save a different version of a presentation while keeping the original, you can create a copy. For example, if you have a file named Client Presentation you can save it as Client Presentation 2 so you'll be able to edit the new file and still refer back to the original version. To do this, you'll click the Save As command in the backstage view. Just like when saving a file for the first time, you'll need to choose where to save the file and give it a new file name.

Running a Presentation-

Most PowerPoint presentations are created to run as a slideshow. Given all the advanced features available in PowerPoint 2010, it is no surprise that there are many features related to running the slideshow that has been included in this program too. Most of these features are really to help you create a good slideshow without having to go through the entire presentation over and over again after every minor change. Features related to running the slideshow are grouped under the Slideshow ribbon.

Closing a Presentation-

Closing a presentation is certainly easier than opening one. To close a presentation, save your file and use one of these techniques:

- Click the Office button and choose Close on the drop-down list. The PowerPoint program remains open, although the presentation is closed.

- Click the Close button, the X in the upper-right corner of the PowerPoint window (or press Alt+F4). Clicking the Close button closes PowerPoint as well as your presentation.

Opening an Existing Presentation-

PowerPoint and Windows offer many shortcuts for opening an existing presentation. To open a presentation, click the Office button and choose Open - or take advantage of the numerous ways to open presentations quickly as-

- Click the Office button and choose Open on the drop-down list (or press Ctrl+ O). You see the Open dialog box.
- Locate and select the presentation you want to open and then click the Open button. You can also double-click a presentation name to open a presentation.

POINTS TO REMEMBER:

- Microsoft PowerPoint is widely used for making professional quality presentations in a variety of formats, including on-screen computer slide shows, black-and-white or color overheads, and 35 mm slides. You can also use it for notes and class presentations. In addition, PowerPoint can be used as a drawing package for preparing pictures, forms, posters and leaflets.
- Presentation is a powerful managerial tool of communication through which you can compile and deliver your ideas, concepts, plans and products to the audience in a structured, effective and impressive manner.
- Slides and transparencies are used to projected in front of the audience using an overhead projector or otherwise. The operation of this equipment was mainly manual, semi-automated at best.

GLOSSARY:

- Title Bar: This is the top section of the window. It shows the name of the file followed by the name of the program, which in this case is Microsoft PowerPoint.
- Slide Area: This is the area where the actual slide is created and edited. You can add, edit and delete text, images, shapes and multimedia in this section.
- Normal Layout View: This displays page in normal view with the slide on the right and a list of thumbnails to the left. This view allows you to edit individual slides and also rearrange them.
- Slide Tab: This section is available only in the normal view. It displays all the slides in sequence. You can add, delete and record slides from this section.
- Quick Access Toolbar: The Quick Access Toolbar is located just under the ribbon. This toolbar offers a convenient place to group the most commonly used commands in PowerPoint.

CHAPTER SEVEN

FUNDAMENTALS OF INTERNET

INTRODUCTION:

Internet is also known as 'THE NET'. The internet is a global wide area network that connects computer system across the world. It includes high-bandwidth data lines that comprise the internet's "backbone". The net comes up with different duties:

- Web- Collection of web pages.
- Email- Method of sending and receiving messages online.
- Social Media- That allows people to connect through texts, photos, etc.
- Online Gaming-Simply the gaming things that one can play online. Earlier people used dial up modems to play games on the internet. Nowadays, one can play games easily with friends on devices like mobile phone, etc.

APPLICATIONS OF INTERNET:

- Communication- Internet allows us to communicate with people through videos, photos, documents, etc. With the help of internet people send or receive items. They're able to communicate better no matter how far they're with each other. Internet telephony is another common communication service that is made possible through internet.

- Job Search- Companies post advertisement on newspaper but it's not necessary that each and every one who wants job will receive it. Internet provides us that facility in the job like the companies who need employees can register themselves. Likewise, job seekers can get to know about them more quickly.
- Online Shopping- Online shopping is a trend nowadays as it allows people to shop online by just sitting at your home or anywhere. They also provide product information. For example- Amazon, Flipkart, Ebay, etc.
- Research- Research papers are present online, which helps in the researchers do literature review.
- Video Conferencing- It enables user's direct face-to-face communication across networks via web cameras, microphones, and other communication tools.
- Stock Market Updates- One can sale out or purchase the items while sitting at home through internet.
- Reservation-One can also book tickets for movie or flights or anything via internet.

CONNECTING TO THE INTERNET:

1. On the Source of Internet-

While connecting to the internet the very first step is to make sure that the source of internetmust be on. This is one of the most common mistake people make while connecting.

1. See Your Network Setting-

The very next step is to go to your network setting and adjust it accordingly. This process is somewhat varying in different devices, but the most thing you have to keep in your mind is to access the network setting. Some common devices or operating systems, and their paths to the settings, are listed below.

- Windows XP: Start –> Control Panel –> Network and Internet Connections
- Windows Vista: Start –> Network –> Network and Sharing Centre
- Windows 7: Start –> Control Panel –> Network and Internet
- Windows 8: Start –> Search "View network connections" –> View Network Connections
- Windows 10: Search "View network connections" –> View Network Connections
- Mac OS X Jaguar and later: System Preferences –> Network
- Ubuntu and Fedora: Network Manager
- iOS (iPhone, iPad, etc.): Settings –> Wi-Fi
- Android: Settings –> Wi-Fi (or Wireless & Networks)
- Windows phone: Settings –> Wi-Fi

3. Connecting Using Wireless Broadband-

Go to the internet option>connect to the network, then select wifi . The wifi networks ask for password, type and connect.

4. Connecting Using an Ethernet Cable-

Many recent devices can connect directly to the router. However, laptops for example cannot. Because they do not have any component we can connect via adapter. Ethernet cables are all different; for example, a Cat-5 or Cat-5e cable runs at slower speeds than a Cat-6. Connect one end of the cable to the computer and one end to the broadband. Go to network setting and adjust in accordingly.

BASICS OF COMPUTER NETWORK:

Computer network is a set of computers that are connected together for sharing information. The most common resource shared today is connection to the Internet. A computer network is a set of connected computers. Computers on a network are called nodes. Several computer can be connected together via cable usually (Ethernet cable) or wirelessly (through radio waves).

Computer Network Components-

Here are essential computer network components:

- **Switches**: Switches work as a controller which connects computers, printers, and other hardware devices to a network in a campus or a building. It allows devices on your network to communicate with each other as well as with other networks. It helps you to share resources and reduce the costing of any organization.

- **Routers**: Routers help you connect with multiple networks. It enables you to share a single internet connection with multiple devices and saves money. This networking component acts as a dispatcher allowing you to analyze data sent across a network. It automatically selects the best route for data to travel and send it on its way.

- **Servers**: Servers are computers that hold shared programs, files, and a network operating system. Servers allow access to network resources to all the users of the network.

- **Clients**: Clients are computer devices that use the network as well as shared network resources. They are also users of the network, as they can send and receive requests from the server.

- **Transmission Media**: Transmission media is a carrier used to interconnect computers in a network, such as coaxial cable, twisted-pair wire, and optical fiber cable. It is also known as links, channels, or lines.

- **Access points**: Access points allow devices to connect to the wireless network without cables. A wireless network allows you to bring new devices and provides flexible support to mobile users.

- **Shared Data**: Shared data are data which is shared between the clients such as data files, printer access programs, and email.

- **Network Interface Card**: Network Interface card sends, receives data, and controls data flow between the computer and the network.

- **Local Operating System**: A local OS helps personal computers to access files, print to a local printer and uses one or more disk and CD drives are located on the computer.

Types of Network-

Local Area Network (LAN)-

- The full form of LAN is Local Area Network.
- IT is basically a group of networks that are connected together in a small area.
- Its setup is cheaper.
- It provides high security.
- Data is transferred at high speed.
- Example-building, school etc.

Metropolitan Area Network (MAN)-

- The full form of MAN is Metropolitan Area Network.
- It covers a region larger than covered by LAN.
- It is used to mean the interconnection of several local area networks by bridging them with backbone lines
- Example-large universities, cities, etc.

Wide Area Network (WAN)-

- The full form of WAN is Wide Area Network.
- It is bigger than the LAN.
- It extends over large areas like cities.
- Internet is one of the biggest WAN in the world.
- Examples-mobile broadband, private network.

MISCELLANEOUS ABOUT INTERNET BASICS:

Understanding URL

The full form of URL is Uniform Resource Locator. It is basically the address of a resource on the internet and indicates the location of a resource as well as the protocol. A URL contains the following information:

- The protocol used to access the resource
- The location of the server (whether by IP address or domain name)
- The port number on the server (optional)
- The location of the resource in the directory structure of the server
- A fragment identifier (optional)
- An example of URL is https://www.amazon.com, which is the URL for the amazon website.

A domain name is a part of URL:

Overview of URL:

Below is the additional information about each of the sections of the http URL:

- http:// or https://: The "http" stands for Hypertext Transfer Protocol. It lets the browser to know which protocol it is going to use to access the information specified in the domain.
- www: "www" stands for World Wide Web and is used to distinguish the content.
- Computerhope.com: "computerhope.com" is the domain name for the website. It is used to identify the type or location of the website.
- jargon/u/: The "jargon" and "u" portions of the above URL are the directories where the web page is located on the server.
- url.htm: url.htm is the actual web page on the domain you're viewing.

Search Engine-

A web search engine or Internet search engine is a software system, designed to carry out web search, i.e., to search the World Wide Web in a systematic way for particular information specified in a textual web search query.

OR

Search engine is a website for the user to search the content of internet. User just has to put the searching item into the search bar as shown below

How does the search engine work?

CRAWL: Scour the Internet for content, looking over the code/content for each URL they find.

INDEX: Store and organize the content found during the crawling process. Once a page is in the index, it's in the running to be displayed as a result to relevant queries.

BLANK: Provide the pieces of content that will best answer a searcher's query, which means that results are ordered by most relevant to least relevant.

Internet as an educational tool

Internet is not only beneficial for communication and entertainment but also incredibly useful for educational purposes.

Accessibility-

- Some universities have opened free courses on a variety of subjects. Such as- Harvard, Stanford, MIT, etc.
- These online lectures consist of not only notes but also videos.

Communication-

- If there is a student who has a missed class. Internet allows instantaneous communication between teachers and one's classmates.
- People working together on a project or something are able to connect more easily via internet.

Study and Research-

The internet contains information on wide variety of topics one can even think of. You can search and research about anything of your choice. Internet is the largest encyclopaedia consisting large amount of information about each and every topic.

POINTS TO REMEMBER:

- The Internet is generally defined as a global network connecting millions of computers. More than 100 countries are linked into exchanges of data, news and opinions.

- The Internet is a massive network of networks, a networking infrastructure. It connects millions of computers together globally, forming a network in which any computer can communicate with any other computer as long as they are both connected to the Internet.
- The World Wide Web, or simply Web, is a way of accessing information over Internet. It is an information-sharing model that is built on the top of Internet.
- No one actually owns the Internet or any person or organization controls the Internet in its entirety. Internet is more of a concept than an actual tangible entity, and it relies on a physical infrastructure that connects networks to other networks.

GLOSSARY:

- LAN: The computers are geographically close together (i.e., in the same building).
- MAN: The computers are farther apart and are connected (i.e., in the same city).
- WAN: The computers are farther apart and are connected (i.e., not in the same city).
- Topology: The geometric arrangement of a computer system. Common topologies include a bus, star, and ring. Hybrids of these are star bus & star ring.
- Protocol: The protocol defines a common set of rules and signals that computers on the network use to communicate.
- Switches: Switches work as a controller which connects computers, printers, and other hardware devices to a network in a campus or a building.
- Routers: Routers help you to connect with multiple networks. It enables you to share a single internet connection with multiple devices and saves money.
- Clients: Clients are computer devices which access and uses the network as well as shares network resources.
- Servers: Servers are computers that hold shared programs, files, and the network operating system. Servers allow access to network resources to

all the users of the network.

- Transmission Media: Transmission media is a carrier used to interconnect computers in a network, such as coaxial cable, twisted-pair wire, and optical fiber cable. It is also known as links, channels, or lines.
- Network Interface Card: Network Interface card sends, receives data, and controls data flow between the computer and the network.

CHAPTER EIGHT

INTRODUCTION TO E-COMMERCE

INTRODUCTION:

In our day to day life, we perform various tasks with the help of Internet like purchasing or selling goods. Electronic commerce or e-commerce is basically the exchange of information/currency for goods or services online.

The term e-commerce got popularized from the 1980s, where it denotes the buying and selling of goods through the transmission of data, made possible by the introduction of the electronic data interchange (EDI). In the current digital society, e-commerce can be viewed as online business, becoming one of the most popular method of making money online and an attractive opportunity for the investors.

Sharing business information, maintaining business relationships and conducting business transactions using computers connected to a telecommunication network is called E- Commerce. A more general definition of e-commerce is given by Wigand (1997) as, "The seamless application of information and communication technology (ICT) from its point of origin to its endpoint along the entire value chain of business processes conducted electronically and designed to enable the accomplishment of a business goal. These procedures may be partial or complete or may encompass business to business as well as business to consumer and consumer to business transactions."

Originally, e-commerce means the facilitation of commercial transactions electronically, using technology such as Electronic Data

Interchange (EDI) and Electronic Funds Transfer (EFT). These were both introduced in the late 1970s, allowing businesses to send commercial documents like purchase orders or invoices electronically. The growth and acceptance of credit cards, automated teller machines (ATM) and telephone banking in the 1980s were also forms of e-commerce strongly and changed the old conceptions of e-commerce. Now, the new age e-commerce has spread to areas like airline reservation system, railway reservation system, online shopping, online business and many more. The e-commerce means the use of Internet and the web for business transactions/commercial transactions, which typically involves the exchange of values/information/ ideas across organizational or individual boundaries.

It is a process of purchasing, selling, shifting or exchanging products, services, and or information via electronic networks and computers. E-commerce is like a parasol that covers everything there is to do with purchasing or selling online. It can sometimes be written as "E Commerce", "e-commerce", or eCommerce". The term commerce is defined as trading of good & services; 'e' for 'electronic' is added to this, e- commerce in simpler terms can be defined as trading of goods, services, information or anything else of value between two entities over the internet. Following are some definitions of e-commerce-

- It is the ability to conduct business electronically over the internet.
- It means managing transactions using networking and electronic means.
- It is a platform for selling products & services via internet.

WHY E-COMMERCE?

Application of digital technologies to business processes within the firm is called e-business. These technologies have deep impact on commerce more than e-commerce. E-commerce technology is powerful than any other technology which has left economic effect on the world. The evolving internet and other technologies are bound to shape the 21st century. The traditional process of marketing and sales was a lengthy process of selling and advertising. Branding required long term product observation of the customers. Selling was done through well-insulated channels in a traditional manner limited by social and geographical boundaries. Information about the product was not available everywhere, creating profitable information asymmetries. It was difficult to change the national or regional prices in traditional retailing. One national price was a norm and different regions had different prices for the same product. E-commerce has challenged this traditional thinking.

Some key Features of e-commerce are-

- Ubiquity- It is available everywhere at any time. The result is called a market space, a marketplace extended beyond traditional boundaries and removed from a temporal and geographic location. It saves transaction cost and time. In traditional commerce, you have to visit physically to a market place, in contrast, you do not have to visit anywhere for e-commerce market.
- Global reach- Due to e-commerce technology, commercial transactions has crossed all the cultural and national boundaries whereas traditional commerce are unable to cross- national boundaries.
- Universal Standards- E-commerce has become universal. It is shared by all the nations. While traditional technologies differ from one nation to the next. For the merchant's market entry cost is same all over the world and it is lowered due to internet. For the customers price and product search is lowered. Prices are constant throughout the world and can be searched from any part of the world.
- Richness- Information about any product is easily available. Traditional markets, national sales forces and retail stores are able to provide the prompt audio and visual information, which makes it a powerful selling and commercial environment. Exchange of information and goods is not distance dependent. The richness of a message is spread evenly i.e. complexity and the content of the message is same throughout the world.
- Interactivity- It allows two-way communications between merchant and customer, no other commercial technology of the 20th century except telephone has this feature. E- commerce can be used using different websites for both giving and receiving the information from the net.
- Information Density- Information available on the web is more accurate and reaches the person fast in a timely manner. The information is complete and is available to all consumers, merchants and participants.

- Customization- E-commerce technologies allow personalization by targeting their marketing message to a specific person by adjusting a message to person's name, interests, and past purchases. Technology also permits customization by changing the product according to the user's requirement. A lot of information about the customer's requirement, its past purchases can be stored due to information density.

Importance of e-commerce-

SETUP: The set-up of E-commerce is much easier than a physical setup including cost and everything.

MORE INFORMATION: Customers can get more information regarding the product they're looking for like all the details regarding the product is given in the description column of a product.

REVIEWS: People while buying things online can also get reviews regarding the products so they can get the clear idea of the products whether it's of use or not .

LESSER COST: If the inventory management of goods and services is an automated process then not only there will be a reduction in costs, but also in risk. Also, having e-commerce business is much more cost effective than a physical store as it saves your extra expenses like rent, electricity, etc.

Applications of e-commerce-

Marketing: E-commerce helps in marketing activities such as fixation of price, negotiation, product feature enhancement and relationship with the customer.

Finance: Nowadays, most companies use e-commerce to a greater extent. Customers can perform a lot of tasks through online banking or E-commerce such as- check balances or savings, pay bills and so on.

Manufacturing: E-commerce can be used in the chain operations of a company. Some company form an electronic exchange by providing both buying and selling of goods, trade market information and run-back office information such as inventory control.

Online Publishing: It includes the digital publication of e-books, digital magazines, and the development of digital libraries.

Auctions: It also includes auctions that involve bidding. Bidding is a special type of auction that allows prospective buyers to bid for an item.

TYPES OF E-COMMERCE MODELS:

Before we check the different e-commerce business models, let us briefly discuss the types of e-commerce business classifications. With the rise in popularity of e-commerce, people are increasingly finding themselves thinking about opening online businesses. E-commerce models can be categorized into following categories.

- Business to business(B2B)
- Business to consumer(B2C)
- Consumer to consumer(C2C)
- Consumer to business(C2B)
- Business to government(B2G)
- Consumer to government(C2G)

a. BUSINESS TO BUSINESS (B2B)- B2B, or Business to Business, is the largest e- commerce model. In this model, both the sellers and buyers are business entities. This model describes the transactions between a retailer or a wholesaler, or a wholesaler and manufacturer. Also, the transaction of the B2B business model is much higher than that of the B2C model. In this model, the products are being sold to an intermediate buyer who then sells the product to the final customer. As younger generations enter the age of making business decisions, B2B selling in the online space is becoming more important. Some of the examples of B2B models are Alibaba (world's largest online business to the business trading platform), Amazon business, IBM, Boeing, ExxonMobil Corporation, and more.

b. BUSINESS TO CONSUMER (B2C) - In this model, the product is being sold to the end user. It is one of the most common use business models. Business to consumer, known as B2C, is the most common and the thickest e-commerce market. In this model, the decision-making process is shorter than B2B model. The B2C business is the most common type. This is the thickest e-commerce market. In this online model, the business sells to individual customers. This business model offers direct interaction with customers. Some examples of B2C models are WalMart,

Staples, Target, and REI.

c. CONSUMER TO CONSUMER (C2C) - This model helps consumers to sell their things (assets) like -property, cars, etc., or rent a room by publishing their information on the website Companies like Craigslist and eBay who pioneered this model in the early days of the internet. The C2C or consumer to consumer business model involves a transaction between two consumers. It is also known as a citizen to citizen. A common example of this model would be an online auction, where a customer or visitor posts an item for sale and other customer bids to purchase it. However, the third party generally charges a commission. The few examples for this model include Craigslist, eBay and OLX.

d. CONSUMER TO BUSINESS (C2B)- In this model, consumer process towards a website showing multiple business organizations for a particular service. Customer to business, known as C2B, involves customers selling their services or products to business. It is roughly the same as a sole proprietorship serving a larger business. One thing that differentiates C2B from other business models is that the consumers create the value for the products. The consumer places an estimate of amount he/she wants to spend for a particular service or it allows a customer to sell their products to companies. In this e-commerce model, a site might allow customers to post the work they want to be completed and have businesses bid for the opportunity. Affiliate marketing services would also be considered C2B.C2B examples include Google Adsense, Commission Junction, and Amazon. Fotolia is also emerging as a good C2B example.

e. BUSINESS TO GOVERNMENT (B2G) - It is alternative of B2B model. Such websites are used by governments to trade and exchange information with various business organizations. Business to government is also referred to as the business to administration commerce. In this model, government and businesses use central websites to do business with each other more efficiently than they can off the web. This e-commerce model is also referred as public sector marketing, i.e., marketing services and products to multiple government levels. With this platform, businesses can bid on government opportunities, including tenders' auctions, and application submission.

f. CONSUMER TO GOVERNMENT (C2G) - Consumer to administration or consumer to government e-commerce model enables the consumers to post feedback or request information regarding public sectors directly to the government administration or authorities. For example, when you pay electricity bill through government websites, payment of health insurance, make payment of taxes, etc.

ADVANTAGES OF E-COMMERCE:

- Messages and important information can reach the world in no time which makes the process effective and cheap for suppliers and customers.
- An online store works 24 hours a day, 7 days a week, 365 days a year or via an EDI system.
- The costs required to set up offices is very high in comparison with the cost of setting an e-commerce website which in turn can be integrated with less efforts.
- New market segments can be explored with the use of Internet.
- Business processes are automated and with increased efficiencies there is no need to re- key in orders into order entry system.
- Easy search of required quality product with wider choice range and no wastage of time.
- Easy Buying/selling of items with the use of Internet using a computer.
- Use of financial and legal services, medical advice etc. from proper portals.
- No need of personal visit and searching. Large variety of goods accessible easily without spending time and money.

POINTS TO REMEMBER:

- Commerce is defined as trading of good & services or if e 'for electronic' is added to this, the definition of e-commerce becomes the trading of goods, services, information or anything else of value between two entities over the internet.
- E-Commerce or Electronics Commerce is a methodology of modern business, which addresses the need of business organizations, vendors

and customers to reduce cost and improve the quality of goods and services while increasing the speed of delivery.

- EDI is an electronic data interchange. It is the direct communication of trading messages between computer systems, using national and international telecommunications networks.

GLOSSARY:

- B2B: The process of selling services or products to another business, which typically then sells to the consumer.
- B2C: The process of selling services or products directly from the business to the consumer
- Domain: The main page or main URL for a website. This is often the 'homepage' or the root portion of the web address.
- Mobile Commerce: The process of buying products or services on a mobile or wireless handheld device.
- Transaction: Purchasing an order online from a business or other seller.

CHAPTER NINE

E-OFFICE MANAGEMENT TOOLS

INTRODUCTION

E-office or electronic office is a term that refers to any office environment that makes significant use of computer technology to operate. The term was first coined during the middle of the 20th century and began to come into common use during the decade of the 1980s as more office environments dispensed with manual methods and began to rely more heavily on a combination of desktop computers, mainframes, and servers to manage a number of job-related tasks. Today, electronic office is more commonly equated with a virtual office, which involves the use of wireless technology allowing people to work from virtually anywhere with the right type of laptop or notebook and a reliable wireless connection.

WHY E-OFFICE?

For decades, paper documents and filing cabinets have been the way to organize information in an office, or at home. But that doesn't mean they're the best option. Many offices and homes globally are transitioning from physical documents to electronic document management. Why do they want to go paperless? Well, there are many reasons to get started for going paperless in today's modern business climate.

More and more business people are starting to realize that paper is an expensive and inefficient way to manage their information. So, they turn to a service, like electronic document management which has the tools they need. But going paperless isn't something that happens overnight; it is a process that takes time and effort, and many business owners and at home workers are intimidated by the prospect of making the switch.

As intimidating as the concept may be, going paperless with information management systems is a necessity if you're going to compete in the modern business world and still have a life outside the office.

Lead the Way-

What do you think is the number one reason why companies aren't going paperless? The answer may surprise you.47% of employees surveyed said that one of the top three reasons for not going paperless was a lack of management initiatives or mandates. Essentially, they're ready and willing to go paperless, but nobody is leading the way or providing the tools. Executing steps for going paperless means your home business and major company needs you to take the initiative, step up, and lead the way for a more efficient office. Your employees will be grateful for improving their life at work.

Here are some tips for going paperless. Set goals for each department and for the company as a whole that encourage everyone to transition to an electronic document management system. You may even want to set up some kind of reward initiative for when the goal is met to encourage employees to participate in the efforts to go paperless.

The important thing about going paperless is that you lead by example. If you have your own Filing cabinet of documents, take responsibility for transitioning those to an electronic system. Set goals for yourself, and take ownership for meeting those goals. If your employees see you leading the way, they are more likely to follow, and you'll drive home how important going paperless really is.

Get Everyone on Board with Going Paperless-

No matter how strong the paperless example you set, your company won't make the transition unless you have your employees on board. Make sure the employees know about mobile apps. It gives them easy access wherever they have phone service. They can view, read, and share documents and files without taking up any personal phone storage. A recent survey asked businesses which departments were most resistant to a paperless work environment. It was found that legal and finance departments tend to be the most hesitant about going paperless. So how can you get them and the rest of your teams started and on board with the paperless plan? Here are three tips that might help.

- Show them the ways going paperless benefits them: Demonstrate to people how going paperless will make their jobs easier. If they see the time and effort they can save, they're more likely to be on board with going paperless.

- Address compliance concerns about going paperless: There's a reason legal and finance department are the most resistant to go paperless: they're worried about compliance issues. However, the truth is going paperless can actually help you to become more compliant. Paper processes expose your company to potential liability due to lack of security or lost paperwork. On the other hand, electronic document management software possesses security measures and other features that ensure vital information is protected. Demonstrate these digital features to your team members to show them how going paperless not only doesn't create compliance issues but can actually eliminate potential issues in existing paperless processes.

- Show how going paperless benefits customer services: The majority of consumers today prefer electronic correspondence to paper correspondence because they are easier to handle and are more secure. Providing these kinds of digital services for your customers can get a lot of your team members on board with the switch because customer service is arguably the most important part of any business.

Organize your Paper Documents and Files-

Now that you've set up some initiatives and gotten your team on board for going paperless, it's time to start the dirty work. Before you begin scanning your physical documents into their new home in the digital cloud, an electronic system, read these ways to organize what you have—and odds are, you have a lot. To tackle these mounds of paper documents, you should divide the work and utilize your team appropriately.

Here's how you can quickly and easily get your stacks of paper documents organized and ready to be entered into a digital system on a desktop computer or in the cloud. Once the paper documents are all organized, you can prepare to take your business, whether at home or in a corporate office, into the paperless era.

Get Software and Get Training-

While your employees are preparing their documents and files for entry, you need to find the right digital document management system to aid you going paperless. There are many digital document management systems out there for you to choose from, so you need to do your research and compare your options before making a decision. To help you during your search, you should sit down and make a list of the tools you need in a DMS service, as well as the things you want that aren't absolute necessities. These typically involve data backup, amount of storage, number of user accounts, audit logs, employee permissions, and automation.

Once you've read the tips and created a list of necessary tools, you need to figure out your budget for the new office software. You may need to consult with the finance team about this. Then, with your list in hand and budget in mind, you can start comparing cloud document management software. You should aim to find something that meets all of your needs and at least a few of your wants while still staying in your budget.

Get as many demonstrations and trials as you can so you can see how the software functions. You may want to let other employees test the software, to ensure that it is usable and easy to learn by others in the office.

After selecting your software, you need to select the office employees who need to be trained on the best way to use it. Depending on your situation and your business, you may want only certain departments to learn how to use the software or only the leaders of certain departments. The important thing is that all employees who handle, file, and need access to information in the cloud will be able to do so digitally and confidently.

Get Started Right the Way and File Electronically-

One of the most important tips for going paperless is relying on the right scanner to make the transition. With the necessary employees trained in the software, you can start scanning in your documents and filing them electronically with a document management vendor's scanner selection. This is also a good time for you to assess how to handle incoming documents and digital files while catching up on your backlog of existing documents. From the time you scan your first document; all incoming paperwork should be filed electronically. After all, you don't want to be constantly playing "catch-up" when it comes to being paperless; you want to move forward with paperless processes already in place.

Tell Clients, Tips, and Share Electronically-

Once you have your current documents switched to electronic copies, you can't stop there. Tell your clients about the switch you've made. Make sure to send out an email addressing any security concerns, and tell them about all of the benefits they'll experience from the switch. You'll also want to introduce them to electronic sharing as well. If your clients at home sharing digital documents with you and sign documents electronically with a phone or computer, your company will save even more time and money.

Make sure your clients are familiar with whatever version of electronic sharing you choose to use- email, online sharing, etc. Be willing to answer their questions and provide tips to make the transition easier for them. Any tips or help will let your clients know you care about their success.

One of the most important steps for going paperless is also to introduce them to the electronic signature services as well. Get your clients started with as many paper-free processes as you can. You will also help your company to keep your paperless systems consistent, efficient, and organized on your computer.

Enjoy the Benefits-

Once you finish the steps for going paperless, much less effort is needed to ensure you stay paperless, so you'll be able to rest on your laurels for a bit. Mostly you should minimize printing from a computer, and maintain the consistency in naming and filing.

As you continue to use a computer to make your processes digital, you'll see a number of benefits in your office and life outside of work. With savings in time and cost, as well as increased document security, data backup, your employees, customers, and your business as a whole will benefit from making the switch to a paperless office. When people at home or work ask how you had such a great business year, feel free to share these tips. After all, our main goal as a company is to improve your life by reducing stress at work.\

BASIC INFRASTRUCTURE & PRE-REQUISITES FOR E-OFFICE:

Basic infrastructure-

Digital workplaces not only enhance employee experience but enable business excellence and cost arbitrage. Research has shown that 87% of CIOs believe that digitally empowering employees can drive at least 5% additional revenue growth over three years (2). Here's a deeper look into some of these digital workplace infrastructure use cases that have already found a way into offices and are making an impact:

1. **User Preference-based Lighting and Temperature Control**

Two of the most basic office necessities are lighting and air-conditioning/temperature control. An 'ideal temperature' is a myth. Employees have varied temperature requirements, which often lead to office temperature debates. This never-ending temperature tussle could be solved with the help of technology. Some companies have employed applications that allow employees to provide feedback on the current temperature – 'I'm cold,' 'It's too hot!', or 'It's perfect.' Based on such inputs, the building facility management team can adjust the temperature. Such tools place the control in the employee's hand, which further boosts productivity and employee satisfaction. A step further is a technology that helps employees set preferred temperatures for their own bays/work desks.

Similarly, for lighting, companies are exploring ways to install connected lighting systems that allow for remote light controlling, offering energy savings in the process. For instance, Cisco partnered with Philips to jointly implement smart lighting and HVAC systems. Philips' connected lighting system collected data from 600 PoE (Power over Ethernet) enabled luminaries equipped with sensors to capture temperature, light level, and activity for optimizing user comfort. Philips' lighting management software, running in the building's IT environment, allowed system managers to monitor and manage each light point via a dashboard application. The system also stored data over time, allowing managers to assess occupancy patterns and optimize lighting operations based on historical trends and findings. Cisco thus reduced energy consumption in its office spaces and had better control of the lighting system.

2. Digital Building Management System

A digital building management system will help enable facilities managers to run their buildings with high service levels and deliver cost savings and environmental benefits through reduced power consumption. For instance, a bank implemented technologies that help merge isolated building systems such as sensors, lighting, HVAC, security, and audio-video into a single system. It brought together different building systems on a single IP in order to be monitored and managed more effectively.

3. Intelligent Workspace Allocation

Several companies today have implemented intelligent workspace allocation systems, which allow employees to choose and block their workstation based on their requirement for the day. Employees can also block workstations for longer durations, per their needs. This gives employees the freedom to select the seats they prefer, based on convenience, amenities required, and the type of work they are engaged in. It also allows employers to track workspace utilization and use the gathered data to plan for future expansion if needed.

Companies are also installing desks with a height adjustment option that enables employees to work either standing or sitting, according to their comfort. Another variant of this is the treadmill desk, where a low torque treadmill is placed below a standing desk, where the employees can walk while working. This improves the overall health of the employees and helps attract the millennial workforces who prefer an ergonomic workplace.

4. 3D Holographic Telepresence

As companies continue to globalize and expand across diverse geographical locations, connecting digitally for meetings and town halls will be key to saving valuable time and traveling cost for leaders as well as organizations. High-definition 3D holograms are one of the most promising technology use cases that can enable these digital meetings. Accenture's tech team has already created a 3D holographic telecast technology to enable the digital presence of leadership teams in key meetings without actually needing them to be physically present. Accenture has built seven studios with the capacity to capture holograms across the globe and plans to expand its use. 3D holograms will not just help increase an organization's efficiency but will also help build a digital-ready culture in the organization.

5. Smart Writing Boards

In several MNCs, traditional whiteboards are being replaced by smart boards. These smart boards can replicate the content onto a laptop or tablet in real-time, enabling better collaboration and saving the time spent on replicating the content. Smart writing boards can be used to edit existing files (e.g. Excel/PPTs) and can be saved for further use as well. Multiple files can be accessed simultaneously at the tap of a finger. Smart boards also have in- built webcams that relay the content being written on the board to a remote location of choice, in real-time. It helps extend the scope of discussions with ease of swapping data through files and making discussions more effective. It also ensures that the points discussed during meetings are captured without any loss of data due to human interventions.

6. Intelligent Amenities

Companies are conscientiously taking initiatives and investing heavily in providing intelligent amenities to the employees through facilities like smart elevators, IoT-enabled parking availability tracking, biometric access and security, interactive platforms, etc. A case in point is RMZ Corp., a commercial real estate company that has adopted technology to transform its tenants' experience by providing them with a highly interactive platform enabled by AI and IoT. The platform acts as a comprehensive productivity and efficiency enabler that allows employees within the campus to enjoy certain features. Employees can make workplace decisions such as the right time and mode to get to and from work, in- campus services, security, concierge services, community socializing, etc.

Pre-requisites for e-office-

Some of the basic requirements for the E-office establishment are given below, e.g. Hardware, Software, Training, actualization.

<u>Actualization</u>

- Pre-transition Preparedness
- Creation of Database (EMD)
- Creation of NIC email ID
- Procurement of Digital Signatures
- Establish a ten member PMU that can be reduced to five after six months and three after one year
- R and I section to be equipped and trained
- User PC Peripheral Equipment modifications
- Scanning
- Self
- Outsourced
- Migration
- All new files as e-files
- Physical files to be migrated to Electronic Files
- Cutoff Date
- Hardware
- Creation of a separate instance
- NIC Network
- Sufficient Bandwidth
- Backend Management Support
- Monitors are not too small
- Adequate RAM in CPU

<u>Strategy</u>

- Setting Up
- Application procurement
- Hardware changes (Screen size & RAM) rollout

- Training
- Scanning Arrangement –Vendor & Officers PA
- Pre-transition preparedness Cut off
- R&I going electronic
- New files electronic

Software

- E-office a NIC developed Software
- E-office Premium and E-office Lite
- Advantages
- File management
- Tracking
- Expeditious Movement
- Location agnostic saves paper
- Saves Space increases transparency
- Leave Management
- Inter Organizational Communication
- Needs to be purchased-Cost varies based on number of users and Locations

Training

- Overview
- Introductory training
- Enablement training
- Learn while you do

COMPONENTS OF E-OFFICE:

Addition, maintenance of certain basic records, scheduling, processing summarized business information for structured decision making, and what-if analyses are some of the other automated office operations. Some of the common components of E-office are: Word Processor, Electronic Spreadsheet, Business Presentations, Scheduler, and Data Base Management System.

Each of these components is designed to perform a special type of desktop activity. The word processors help in designing documents for internal and external communication. The Electronic spreadsheets are used for analyzing numeric data and performing 'what-if' analysis.

The business presentation component of office suite helps in designing screens for business presentations before customers, investors, shareholders, policymakers, etc. These packages combine graphic facilities and databases to make the presentations accurate, interactive and flexible. Schedulers are packages that help managers in time management.

They record a manager's engagements and maintain dynamic scheduling and recordings. As a result, time management is made more systematic. Information regarding the lean periods and busy periods can be obtained easily.

E-FILE MANAGEMENT SYSTEM:

E-file management or electronic document management is the practice of importing, storing, and managing documents in digital format, e.g. images, documents, etc. To resolve the issues with manual file system someone needs to upgrade into e-filing system that eliminates or minimizes the time spent managing and maintaining paper documents, amount of physical storage space required for paper files, risks of document loss due to fire, water damage, or any other physical damage, etc.

Benefits of an e-filing management system-

E-file management system provides the following advantages-

- Save space and resources otherwise needed for organizing, filing, and storing papers.
- Minimize errors that are likely with manual data entry and filing.
- Permanently preserve documents and information that could otherwise be misplaced or lost.
- Reduce or eliminate expenses for office supplies such as printers, copiers, paper, ink, etc.
- Optimize productivity by eliminating time and effort necessary to search through files for information.
- Improve customer service by speeding up response times.

- Access of official documents to the authorized person irrespective of space and time.

POINTS TO REMEMBER:

- E-office software has been designed with an objective to help reduce the movement of hard copy papers within an organization and integrate various, seemingly unrelated activities within an organization.
- The software is based on open technologies and web-based, which is user-friendly. This facilitates easier deployment over the Local Area Network, Wide Area Network as well as over internet whenever required.
- The user can access the system using standard Internet browser such as Internet Explorer or Netscape after necessary authentication.
- The complete system works with a centralized backend database to store the necessary structured information, keyed in by the user.

GLOSSARY:

- Word Processor: Word processor is software or a device that allows users to create, edit, and print documents. It enables you to write text, store it electronically, display it on a screen, modify it by entering commands and characters from the keyboard, and print it.
- Electronic Spreadsheet: Electronic spreadsheets computerise the traditional layout of any tabulation or complex calculation done with pencil, paper and calculator.
- Data-Base Management System: A database management system (DBMS) is a software package designed to define, manipulate, retrieve and manage data in a database.

CHAPTER TEN

FUNDAMENTALS OF BANKING

INTRODUCTION:

Banking is an essential part of modern economy. The idea behind banking is effective use of money. In general, banking deals with the concept of lending. While making the historical study of our society, we came to know that presence of money lenders is always there, which has now been replaced with the concept of banking. While studying the thoughts of Quran, and Arthashastra of Kautilya, we found one common reference is present in them i.e. the rate of interest. Thus, the same concept has been used by today's modern banking. During the medieval age, the concept of banking was carried out at the individual level, but in modern times it has also included the partnership formulation, i.e. banking of stock market companies.

While making the fundamental study of banking, it has been identified that it is a concept that deals with the facilities like:

- Cash storage
- Credit/Loan facility
- Investment
- Deposit/Withdrawal
- Currency Exchange
- Forex Trading and
- Various other financial transactions.

Banking is the key area which is responsible for the efficient driving of an economy of a country. Somehow one can also say that bank is a link between depositors and borrower, i.e. it accepts deposit from a customer (in certain rate of interest) and credit them to the borrower in certain high rate of interest. This transfer of money between depositor and borrower is done under the regulations of the central bank of a country.

BASICS OF BANKING:

Banks are known as 'bancus' or 'banque' in Latin whereas in English it is termed as bench. A bank is an institution which deals with financial transactions like deposit and withdraw of cash/money. It is also a financial intermediary that involves activities like loaning. Banks are generally regulated with certain rules and regulations due to the heavy influence of banking within a financial system and economy of a country. All banks need to comply to the regulations set by Basel i.e. set of international standards for banking. Most of the authors globally have given some definitions regarding banking; some of them are discussed below.

- F.E. Perry: "The bank is an establishment which deals in money, receiving it on deposit from customers, honouring customer's drawings against such deposits on demand, collecting cheques for customers and lending or investing surplus deposits until they are required for repayment."
- Walter Leaf: "A banker is an institution or individual who is always ready to receive money on deposits to be returned against the cheques of their depositors."
- Dr. Herbert L. Hart: "A banker is one who in the ordinary course of his business, honourscheques drawn upon him by persons from and for whom he receives money on current accounts."
- The Indian Banking Companies Act, 1949: "Banking means the acceptance for the purpose of lending or investment, of deposits of money from the public repayable on demand or otherwise, and withdrawal by cheque, draft, order or otherwise".

Characteristics of Banking-

- Trade in Money: All banks deal with money exchanges like deposit of money in bank or lend or borrow the money from banks.
- Company/Firm/Individual: Bank is an institution which can be operated through a company/firm or an individual by the implementation of certain regulations.
- Providing Advances/ Overdraft: A bank provides money in the form of overdraft/ loans to persons/companies who need it for various assignments.
- Easy methods to operate: A bank is also responsible for providing easy facilities for his customers for depositing /withdrawing money through cheques/drafts, etc.
- Various utility services: A bank is also responsible for implementing or provides various banking facilities to its customers through various technologies.

Banking in Asia

Several governments in Asia after independence soon realized the changes to the market economy and the requirement of supportive development to their banking and financial systems, including considerable capacity building in an area that needed to be re-established almost from scratch. The resulting reform programs designed and aimed at restructuring and modernizing of the components of financial system creating conditions for sustainable economic growths were implemented in the 1990s. The entire era has been divided in two stages.

First stage-

During the first phase in Asia, sovereign currencies began with restrictive monetary politics to curb inflation. As a result, high-interest rate policies and formal and informal restrictions on convertibility were implemented and enforced. High-interest rates, low level of reserves, lack of liquidity, economic and political instability and devaluation continued throughout 1995–96, along with continued dollarization of the financial system and outflow of funds.

Second stage-

Improvements in monetary policies, combining structural and institutional reforms, and reforming fiscal discipline eventually brought economic stability to various regions of Central Asia by the mid of the

1990s. Inflation fell from hyperinflationary levels in 1993 to about 15–20 percent in 1997–98 and reduced the devaluation of local currencies, which remained relatively viable until the 1998 Russian financial crisis. In addition, it was at the end of 1997 that gross domestic product (GDP) began to grow in the gross area.

Banking in India

Modern banking was developed in England and introduced in India by the British government during their rule in India. Naturally, Indian banking system today is almost similar to the concept of banking system of the British government. However, this does not mean that banking system was unknown to India. The essence of banking in India had been present since ancient time. In fact, India was a major contributor in international trade and a major producer of steel, textiles, spices and fine articles during the ancient and medieval age. To refer Manusmriti, the concept of rate of interest and security of loans is present in our nation during ancient age. Arthashastra of Kautilya also mentions the regulation of interest rates, deposits and even exemption in bills. They were called 'Hundies'. The big traders, merchants and moneylenders were called his superior as 'nagarseeth', who held important positions in the Mughal and Maratha reign. They had efficient courier systems and had extensive branches all over India and had also given loans to kings.

However, with its double entry accounting system, the emphasis was on modern banking and deposit by the British. The British rule expanded the stages of development in banking in India. Modern banking promoted indigenous banking.

Stages in the Evolution of Banking in India:

The history of the Indian banking system is divided in three stages:

- Before Independence
- Between 1947-1991
- After 1991 to till date

Before Independence

Banking system in India started with the establishment of Bank of Hindustan in the year 1770 but it has been ceased to operate in 1832. During this period, there is an alliance of three major banks i.e. Bank of

Bengal, Bank of Bombay and Bank of Madras. However, during the British rule, these banks were amalgamated formed as a new bank called Imperial Bank established in 1921 with its network of branches in all over the country (taken over by SBI in 1955). Following banks were established during this period:

- Allahabad Bank (Established in year 1865)
- Punjab National Bank (Established in year 1894)
- Bank of India (Established in year 1906)
- Bank of Baroda (Established in year 1908)
- Central Bank of India (Established in year 1911)

Banking Between 1947-1991

Hilton Young Commission emphasized the need for a separate central bank. As per the commission recommendation, Reserve Bank of India has been established in 1935 and after the Independence it has been nationalized on 1 January 1949. Along with the nationalization of reserve bank, regional rural banks were also introduced in our country on 2 October 1975.

Nationalization of banks has improved the efficiency of the banking system of our country. This has boosted the confidence of the public in our banking system. This nationalization has helped increase funds which may lead the economic growth of our country. After independence, another significant step was taken in 1969 which was to nationalize 14 Indian banks. After this in 1980, six more India banks were also nationalized. This nationalization of banks brought about great changes in the policies, attitudes, procedures, functions and coverage of Indian banks throughout the world. Indian banks are now being ready to become leading international players.

Banking After 1991

After 1991, Indian banking system has shown tremendous growth rate. Liberalization policies introduced by the government have also boosted up the growth of Indian banking system. This tenure is also known as the phase of expansion, consolidation and increment of Indian banking system. This tenure has also been responsible for the entry of private sector in Indian Banking System. As a result RBI has given license to ten private entities (ICICI, HDFC and Axis Bank) for the establishment of banks in India.

At present, the banking system of India is known or termed as Modern Banking Era in India. As per the reports published by Reserve Bank of India (RBI), India's banking sector is sufficiently capitalized and well-regulated. The financial and economic conditions of Indian banking system is far superior and better to any other banking system in another country in the world. After making the study of credit, market and liquidity risk, it has been observed that Indian banks are generally durable and have withstood the global downturn well.

The banking industry of India has recently witnessed the implementation of innovative banking solutions like payments and establishment of small finance banks. The new measures of RBI's may go a long way in helping the restructuring of the domestic banking industry. Establishment of digital payments system in India has evolved the most among 25 countries with India's IMPS(Immediate Payment Service) being the only system at level 5 in the Faster Payments Innovation Index (FPII). Currently, Indian banking system features the following:

- 27 public sector banks.
- 21 private sector banks.
- 49 foreign banks.
- 56 regional rural banks.
- 1562 cooperative banks.
- 94,384 rural cooperative banks and cooperative credit institutions.

<u>Key Developments of Indian Banks-</u>

As per the banking reports of September 2018, government of India has initiated the India Post Payments Bank (IPPB) and opened its branches across all the districts of our country for achieving the objective of financial inclusion. As of May 2018, the equity funding of microfinance companies has grown up at the rate of 39.88 to Rs 96.31 billion (Rs 4.49 billion) in 2017-18 from Rs 68.85 billion (US$ 1.03 billion).

STRUCTURE OF INDIAN BANKING SYSTEM:

Indian banking system has divided in two major schedules: (i) Scheduled Banks (ii) Non- Scheduled Banks.

Scheduled Banks-

The banks which have been scheduled in second scheduled of Reserve Bank of India (RBI) Act, 1934 are known as scheduled banks. As per the schedule, these banks must comply of the following:

- Paid-Up capital and collected funds should not be less than Rs Five Lakhs.
- Any activity of the bank should not affect the interest of the customers.

The banks belong to this category are comprised: (i) Commercial Banks (ii) Cooperative Banks.

Further the commercial banks can be divided under the following:

a. **Public Sector Banks-** Banks which are owned by government (i.e. more than 51% of stake) are known as public sector bank. Currently, there are 21 public sector banks in India from which 19 are nationalized. For e.g. SBI, PNB and BOB are top most leading public sector banks in India.

b. **Private Sector Banks-** Are those banks owned by private individuals or institutions. These types of banks are also listed under Indian companies Act 1956 as a limited company. For e.g. ICICI and HDFC are the top leading private sector banks of our country.

c. **Foreign Banks-** Are those banks which are not listed as an Indian company or organization. These banks are incorporated outside the country and they just have some branches in our country. Finally, we can say they are not operated from our country. Some examples of foreign banks are HSBC, etc.

d. **Regional Rural Banks-** Since the middle of 1970's, Regional Rural Banks came into existence in India. These banks were set up with the specific objective of providing credit and facilities of deposits especially to small and marginal farmers, agricultural labor and artisans and small enterprises. Rural development in respect of agriculture, trade, commerce and industry is the prime responsibility of Regional Rural Banks (RRBs) of India. Banks which are operated at state level but they are governed under the regulations of Reserve Bank of India. Some examples of RRB are Uttarakhand

e. **Gramin Bank etc.**

Non-Scheduled Banks-

The banks which are listed under clause (c) of section 5 of the Banking Regulation Act, 1949 (10 of 1949) are known as Non-Scheduled Banks.

BANKING FUNCTIONALITY:

Banking is the life blood of modern commerce. It has played a very important role in the economic development of all the countries of the world. We cannot think of modern commerce without banking.

Banking is a business. Like any other business, banks are also profit-making organizations. Borrowing and lending constitute the banking business as these are the two basic functions of a bank. It should be noted that banking became out of the need of people for safe place of deposits. Later, banks realized that their business could be made profitable if the money they received was re-lent. Gradually, banks started providing many other services to the people. These are other tasks a modern banker performs. All these functions and services can be classified under primary functions and secondary functions.

Basic functions- The entire banking functionality is divided under the following: (i) Primary Functions (ii) Secondary Functions.

Primary Functions-

Primary functions include accepting deposits, granting loans, advances, cash, credit, overdraft and discounting of bills. Some of the primary functions of banks are discussed below

1. **Accepting Deposits-** The most important activity of a commercial bank is to raise deposits from the public. Those who have surplus income and savings, find it convenient to deposit the amount with the banks.

Depending on the nature of the deposit, the money deposited with the bank also earns interest. Thus, deposits with the bank increase with accrued interest. If the rate of interest is high, the public is motivated to deposit more money with the bank. The bank also has the security of deposited funds. Banks are also called custodians of public money. Originally, money is accepted as a deposit to keep it safe, but since banks use this money to learn interest from people who need money, they share a portion of this interest with depositors. The amount of interest depends on the tenure - the time for which the depositor wants to keep the money with the bank - and the ease of withdrawal. The rule of thumb is: the longer the tenure, the higher the rate of interest, and the lower the ban on withdrawals, the lower the interest. Banks can accept the deposits from various sources like:

- Saving deposits
- Fixed deposits
- Current deposits &
- Recurring deposits

2. Granting Advances/Loans

Another important feature of bank is the granting of loans and advances to their customers. Some types of Advances/Loans are:

- Overdraft
- Cash Credits
- Loans
- Bill Exchanges

Secondary Functions-

Secondary functions include issuing letter of credit, undertaking safe custody of valuables, providing consumer finance, educational loans, etc. Some basic secondary functions of banks are:

- Transfer of Funds from one location to another.
- Collection of Cheques from customers.
- Periodic maintenance of customer data.

- Periodic collections from other sources.

In addition to all above tasks bank has also performs some utility tasks like:

- Issue of Demand Draft and Letter of credits
- Locker facility for customer
- Accounting services for their customers
- Dealing with foreign exchange
- Various social welfare programmes.

TYPES OF ACCOUNT HOLDERS IN BANKS:

Bank accounts are of different types which are used to serve different needs. Also, the usage of accounts depends on our goals, it's always good to put the money into the best account and attain good benefits from it. Doing this allows us to make growth in our money or return from our bank. Basically, the prime objective of banks is to collect money from the public. Therefore, for this purpose accounts are to be opened in the bank. In India, anyone who is legally capable can open an account with a banker. While going through the types there are different types account holders.

Individual Account Holder (Single or Joint)-

An individual can open his/her account in the following two categories:

Single account- It means account could be operated singly mode or an individual can only operate the account.

Joint Account- This kind of account is opened when more than one individual want to operate from the same account. It could be opened in the names of two or more persons. When an individual wants to open joint account with a bank, then a precise set of instructions has to be accepted by all the account holders in writing like which members are entitled to draw cheques from the account, in the event of the death who will be the nominee of the account etc. This document (in written) has to be signed by all the account holders in whose names the joint account has been opened.

Company Account-

A company can also open the account in its name, but the account has been taken care of by company owners.

METHODS OF REMMITTANCES:

Remittance is a process of money transfer. In this process, an individual or group of individuals can use various banking techniques to transfer the money from their accounts to any other account globally. In India, banks offer various kinds of methods to perform remittances some of them are discussed below:

a. **Demand Drafts-** Demand draft is an order made from one bank to another branch of the same bank, for paying the specified amount (mentioned in draft) to an individual in his/her account or in his/her name. As the name suggests a draft is always payable on demand. Banks are authorized to issue a draft at their branch for sending the money from one account to another account or account of another individual. As per the Section 85-A of the Negotiable Instruments Act (Made by the government of India) "Demand draft is an order to pay money, drawn by an office of the bank at another office of the same bank for the amount of money payable to order on demand". An individual can buy a demand draft by paying the amount in advance to the respective bank. After this, bank issues the draft to an individual. The bank also makes the additional charges for providing this service.

b. **Banker's Cheque-** Another service offered by the bank for transferring the money. In this process, a cheque which is payable by a bank itself is payable for a simple cheque which is payable from the funds of a particular customer's account. This is a cheque which is usually received by the bank customer (by paying additional value), the point being that the person receiving the cheque has the security to know that it is payable by the bank and thus not bounced. A banker's cheque or bankers draft is a cheque (or cheque), where the amount is withdrawn directly from a bank's funds from a person's account. This is a negotiable instrument to order and draw all the provisions applicable to the investigation of an order and is valid for six months from the date of issue and may be invalid in actual cases.

c. **Truncated Cheque**- The present system of cheque clearance is paper based; it makes the involvement of exchanging the cheques physically. This exchange of cheques requires a clearing cycle of 3 to 7 days. Generally, most of the cheques are cleared in a cycle of three days, these cycles are long and banks delay the receipt of value by customers.

d. **Electronic Fund Transfer (EFT)** - Electronic funds transfer or EFT refers to the usage of IT enabled services for performing various transactions related with money transfer. This deals with the usage of computer-enabled systems for performing various financial transactions electronically. The EFT is a term which can be further used for a number of different concepts some of them are mentioned below: (i) Transactions initiated by cards i.e. debit/credit. (ii) Electronic cheques i.e. CTS enabled cheques. Electronic fund transfer provides a mechanism for electronic payments of amounts and collections of money. In today's scenario, EFT is one of the safest, secure, efficient and less expensive techniques rather than using of paper cheque payments and collection.

e. **RTGS (Real Time Gross Settlement)** - RTGS is the process of settling the payment of an individual as per his/her order. This is also known as the special fund transfer technique where transfer of money can be done from one bank to another bank as per the permissions of account holder. In this system, transfer of money can be done in real time or gross basis. This system was carried by top three leading banks of India in 1985 but in 2005 this has been raised to 90 banks. This system can be operated by central bank of a country so as per the Indian context RBI (Reserve Bank of India) is responsible for all the financial transactions done under RTGS. Implementation of RTGS is an historical event in the history of Indian economy/banking. This system has been proved as an important mile stone for Indian banking system. One of the major benefits of RTGS system is that it minimizes the settlement risks or making the payment in real time basis. This system is designed to transfer the funds on real time basis i.e. no waiting is required for transferring of money.

f. **NEFT (National Electronic Fund Transfer)** - The NEFT is a nation-wide payment system which allows one-to-one funds transfer between accounts. In this system, an individual account holder can electronically transfer funds from any of the bank's branch to any other individual which had an account with any other bank branch in the country participating in this scheme. This scheme has been initiated in the year 2005 by the Reserve Bank of India. The central bank of India i.e. RBI acts as the custodian for this scheme. It is responsible for resolving all the concern issued raised from this system. Recently, the government of India has raised the working hours for this scheme i.e. on 27*7*365 days (on any time basis).

g. **IMPS (Immediate Payment Service)** - As the name suggests, this system allows the instant payment of money from anywhere and anytime basis. Initially this was the only system which allows the payment between accounts on any time basis but now government has allowed NEFT transaction also to be round the clock or any time basis. One major difference between IMPS and other service like NEFT, in IMPS there is a limitation of certain amount for transfer but it get transfer on real time basis whereas this could not be possible for NEFT i.e. it new some time to get transfer the amount to another's account.

h. **SWIFT (Society for Worldwide Interbank Financial Telecommunication)** - This is a payment body which is acceptable world-wide. The SWIFT system allows the financial systems globally to send and receive information at global level. This is also known as a messaging network which is used by financial institutions to securely transfer the information and instructions through a standard system of codes at global level. In this system, each participating body get an eight- or eleven-digit code for transferring/exchanging the money between them. The important key feature about this system is its global acceptance world-wide. Originally, this system was introduced in 1970's and used at global level or transfer of funds between two or more countries.

TECHNOLOGY IN BANKING:

Technology in Indian banking is already transforming the new concepts and facts in financial services, allowing rapid change in the traditional banking landscape in few years. Involvement of safety features through technology, such as advanced cryptography and biometrics, ensure the protection to banks against scams, and remote applications and also make sure that maximum of your tasks are completed without having to visiting the branch.

Technology in banking has brought up a complete paradigm shift in the present functioning of banks and delivery of banking services to its customers. Days are gone when every banking transaction required a personal visit to the branch. In today's scenario, most of the financial transactions could be done from one's home and customers need not visit the bank branch for doing the same. Growth of technology in the financial sector has expanded due to Internet and mobiles. The IT (Information technology) enabled solutions available today is being leveraged in customer satisfaction, driving automation and many more. Most of the IT initiatives of banks in India started in the late 1990s, or early 2000, with an emphasis on the implementation of core banking solutions (CBS), atomization of bank branches and centralization of all the financial operations in the CBS.

Over the last decade of Indian banking sector, it has been observed that most of the banks are capable of offering technology enabled services. While moving from a manual and scale- constrained environment, it is difficult to predict the adverse scenario where the banking sector was in the era before the reforms, when a simple money deposit or withdrawal of money would require a whole day. Use of ATMs, mobile banking and various online bill payments facilities allowed the customers to complete their tasks by without visiting the branch. Use of the technology in banking services is provided by the term called E-banking as discussed below.

E-Banking-

It is also known as web banking or in common terms "Internet Banking". In 1997, ICICI bank was the only bank in India offering internet banking services. But today, most of the new-generation banks offer the same to their customers. It allows the easy and safe accessing of our banking records on 24*7*365 basis i.e. any time banking. Technically it is the use of networking where all banking systems are connected with each other. Through this a customer can access his saving account as well as other financial details through his computer or mobile phone. E-banking services are provided under the following phases:-

Phase I- Under this all the banking services are offered by bank website itself. The customer needs to register himself to attain these services.

Phase II- Customer can access his bank account details through various devices like smart phone, laptops, desk top etc. Under this scheme, customer can access the various services like checking their account balance, etc by e-banking.

Phase III- Bank allows its customer to use e-banking facilities to operate accounts for funds transfer, bill payments etc by making collaboration with third party.

Benefits of E-banking: E-banking is beneficial for both bank and customers. Some are discussed as follows:

For Banks-

- Less expensive due to reduced transaction costs.
- Less Error.
- Reduced paper work.
- More and effective services to customers.

For Customers-

- It is very convenient to customer to access account details.
- Fast and time saver for customers.
- Any time access for account details.

E-Banking Services-
E-banking services are provided to customers through the following:

- **ATM-** ATM is the automation of the Teller. The first ATM appeared in London in 1967 whereas in India the first ATM was setup in 1987 by HSBC bank in Mumbai. An ATM is an electronic cash dispensing and accepting machine. Banks installed these machines to dispense cash to the bank customers for 24*7*365 basis. For availing ATM services, customer needs to apply for ATM service to the bank and giving a prescribed fee a customer can avail this service. In general, banks make certain restriction in using this service like limitation on cash withdrawal and limit on certain transactions.
- **Debit/ Credit Card-** Debit Card or Credit Card are the two-service provided by the bank to his customers. Both of them are payment card that has been issued to the customers for making the payments. The major difference between Debit and Credit Card is in case of debit card the customer can avail the services of cash withdrawal or payments of bills by using his saving bank account i.e. debit card is linked with customers saving bank account. Whereas credit card also allows the customers to pay for various goods and services or get cash from ATM

machine but after some time the amount has to be repaid to the bank by the customer i.e. one can say it is a type of unsecured loan provided by the bank to his customers as per his credit history/ good will.

- **Mobile Banking-** This is a system when bank would provide its services to his customers through mobile phone/smart phone. Under this service, the user can access his account details through mobile devices and it can also use this to make bill payments or transfer money from one location to other location.
- **E-Wallet(s)** - E-wallet is an e-card concept i.e. a user can use this service by using through online mode. E-wallet is a concept where user can link its saving bank account. In response to this a customer can get a user name and password for sending the payment to respective site. Some popular Wallets are: BHIM (Bharat Interface Money), IRCTC, PAYTM, MOBIWIK, AMAZON PAY, PhonePe, etc.

POINTS TO REMEMBER:

- Banking is a service for deposit or withdrawal of money from the bank for the customer.
- E-banking- When customers are availing all the banking services through online mode it is said to be e-banking.
- NEFT (National Electronic Fund Transfer)- Online service provided by the banks for transferring the money through online mode.
- IMPS (Immediate Payment Service) - Online service provided by the bank for the immediate transfer of money from one customer to another customer.
- E-wallet- Used by the customers for paying money during online shopping, etc.

GLOSSARY:

- SB- Saving Bank Account
- BHIM- Bharat Interface Money
- E-Wallet- Electronic Wallet

- SWIFT- Society for Worldwide Interbank Financial Telecommunication
- ATM- Automation of the Teller
- EFT- Electronic Fund Transfer
- FPPI- Faster Payments Innovation Index.

CHAPTER ELEVEN

OFFICE MEETINGS

INTRODUCTION:

Office meetings are an intrinsic part of running a business. They allow for the business to have a common objective. They also allow every employee and department in the business to know what they should be doing. Essentially, they allow everyone to work towards a common goal. A meeting is important because it helps a group to reach a common decision when urgent and crucial matters need to be discussed and brainstormed through personal interaction. E-mail or conference call may not effectively iron out any issues arising in the office. The objective of a meeting is to provide updates, deliver announcements, solicit feedback, share information and participate in a team environment. Meetings should have a detailed agenda, a time limit and a designated moderator to be effective.

OFFICE MEETINGS:

Meetings can be of various types based on formality, purpose, use, legality, participation and more. Types of meetings are; formal meetings, annual general meetings (AGM), statutory meetings, board meetings, and informal meetings. Meeting or plural form "Meetings" can be defined as; "A gathering of people; as for a business, social, or religious purpose."

We know how important part meetings play in our professional lives. But they also have a significant role in other parts of our life. Meetings can be of various types based on formality, purpose, use, legality, participation and more. However, the main principle of the meeting is remaining common: a gathering of people.

Types of Meetings-

1. **Informative**- the purpose is to give information to the participants about a new scheme, product, etc.
2. **Consultative**- the members are consulted to solve a problem.
3. **Executive**- decisions are taken by those empowered to do so.

In practice, most of the meetings serve more purposes than one. Some additional classifications of meetings are – meeting for negotiation purpose, meeting for giving instructions, etc.

Purposes of Meetings-

The purposes of holding meetings are listed here in a skeleton form:

- To reach a common decision/agreement.
- To solve a problem.
- To understand a situation, exchange ideas and experiences.
- To inform, explain, present ideas.
- To give and get feedback on new ideas.
- To give training.
- To plan and prepare for action.
- To resolve differences and misunderstandings.
- To generate enthusiasm and seek cooperation.
- To review past performance and evaluate it.
- To create a feeling of continuity and solidarity in a body's working.

Advantages of Meetings:

- **Save time:** Since one can meet a number of people at a time, a meeting can save time.
- **Addressing groups:** One can divide the audiences according to their background and need, and address them group by group.

- **Cope with information explosion**: New technology and new regulations are coming thick and fast. Meetings enable us to cope with this situation.
- **Social and emotional support:** Members get personal support from each other when they meet and exchange ideas.
- **Feeling of being consulted:** Members get the feeling that they have been consulted and this is useful in getting their intelligent and willing cooperation.
- **Democratic functioning:** Democracy aims at achieving all people's welfare by all people's involvement. This is possible through meetings.
- **Idea development:** Ideas are systematically cross-fertilized, analyzed and improved by a group.
- **Defusing troublemakers**: By collective constructive forces, troublemakers can be isolated in a meeting and positive action gets going. The opponents of a plan get a forum to voice their opposition, which can be overcome before a group of supportive people.
- **Bolder decisions**: Collectively we can take more adventurous decisions because of united strength.
- **Various interest groups represented**: In a meeting many interest groups can be represented and minorities can also be given due attention.
- **Preventing mistakes:** A meeting helps avoid mistakes by a collective and many-angled focus on issues.

Disadvantages of Meeting:

- **Time-consuming**: Meetings require a number of people to come together at the same time and place. This costs time because other work has to be set aside for the sake of the meeting.
- **Inability to arrive at a decision**: Just as "two heads are better than one," it is also true

that "too many cooks spoil the soup." Multiplicity of views and personal stubbornness of members may prevent a meeting from taking a decision which a chief executive may take alone.

- **Lack of seriousness:** Many meetings suffer from the drawback that members come unprepared and feel that the others will do the thinking and talking. They feel they can take a free ride. "Everybody's job is nobody's job."

- **Inexpert chairing**: Just as an airplane is steered by a pilot, a meeting is piloted by the chairperson. His lack of skill and personal failings/biases may fail a meeting.
- **Expensive:** Meetings are expensive to arrange – they require a place, paperwork, prior communication, and travelling by the attendees.
- **Open to disruption**: A meeting is prone to being disrupted by an element that is opposed to its objective. There are times when one passenger's refusal to adjust himself delays the entire flight. The same for meetings. The spirit of give-and-take may be missing in some participants. In this mechanical age, union is strength, and united work is done by means of meetings. It is estimated that worldwide, millions of meetings are conducted every day, and their number and usefulness is on the rise. That is why although many negative remarks are made about the use of meetings; on the whole we find that meeting is a useful device of collective decision-taking and action.

<u>Meetings can also be classified as follows:-</u>

1. **Management Committee Meetings**

Management Committee meetings are vital to the effective functioning of the committee and its ability to carry out its role. They are the means by which the Committee exercises its collective responsibility for leading the organization.

2. Management Sub-Committee Meetings

Under management sub-committee meetings, some powers may be delegated to members, office bearers or to sub-committees. A sub-committee is a small group of people assigned to focus on a particular task or area, such as finance or personnel. A sub-committee generally makes recommendations to the Management Committee for decision.

3. **General Meetings**

A general meeting is a meeting of a company's shareholders (unlike a board meeting, which is a meeting of the directors). Companies Act 2013 2006 provides the statutory framework for the calling and conduct of general meetings.

4. Annual General Meetings

AGM's are held once a year to assess the trading of the organization over the year. All shareholders are invited to intend the GM but they must be given 21 days notice.

5. Board Meeting

Board meetings are held as often as individual organizations require. They are attended by all directors and chaired by the Chairman of the board.

6. Statuary meeting

Statutory meetings are called so that the directors and shareholders can communicate and consider special reports companies are required by law to hold these statutory meetings.

7. Formal meetings

The rules of conduct of formal meetings are laid dozen in a company's Articles of Association and/or Constitution or Standing Orders. With such meetings, a quorum must be present, i.e. the minimum number of people who should be present to validate the meeting. A formal record of these meetings must be kept, usually by the company secretary.

8. Informal meetings

Informal meetings are not restricted by the same rules and regulations as formal meetings. Such meetings may take the form of brainstorming or discussion sessions where strict agendas may not be necessary and minutes may not be kept. However, it is usually considered good business practice for an agenda to be issued to all members before the meetings so that they can be prepared adequately to make valuable contribution. These meetings are attended by a group of managers who may need to discuss a specific matter, report of progress reports. For example, the marketing manager, sales manager, production manager, and research and development manager may meet to discuss the launch of a new product being launched soon.

9. Celebrations

A celebration is a special enjoyable event that people organize because something pleasant has happened or because it is someone's birthday or anniversary

10. Rituals/Services

A ritual is a sequence of activities involving gestures, words, actions, or objects, performed in a sequestered place and according to set sequence.

NOTICE:

A notice of meeting is a document informing the members or directors of a company about an upcoming meeting. This document specifies the date, time and place of the meeting and the general nature of the business to be transacted at the meeting. When a meeting is to be convened, a notice is required to be sent to all who are to attend it. It should satisfy the following conditions:

a. It should be under proper authority.
b. It should state the name of the organization.
c. It should state the day, date, time, and place. Also, sometimes, how to reach the place.
d. It should be well in advance. Some require seven days notice, some 48 hours.
e. It should state the purpose and, if possible, the agenda.
f. It should carry the date of circulation and convener's/secretary's signature.
g. It should go to all persons required at the meet.
h. It should mention the TA/DA etc. payable and the arrangements for this.

In practice, it is necessary to ensure that the notice has reached in time. This may be done telephonically. Dispatch section and post are prone to delays. We often find that between the date of a letter from a major public organization and the post mark on the letter, there is a gap of 10-12 days. A notice that should reach seven days before a meet should not reach seven days after the meet.

AGENDA:

An agenda is a list of meeting activities in the order in which they are to be taken up, beginning with the call to order and ending with adjournment. It usually includes one or more specific items of business to be acted upon. It may, but is not required to, include specific times for one or more activities. An agenda may also be called a docket, schedule, or calendar. It may also contain a listing of an order of business. Agendas most often include: Informational items - sharing out updates regarding a topic for the group. For example, a manager may provide an update on the year-end planning process. Action items - items that you expect the group will want to review during the meeting.

Types of Agenda

There are a variety of agenda formats; the purpose and type of meeting will determine which agenda format to use. Types of agendas typically include-Informal, formal, prioritized and timed. Familiarizing yourself with each agenda format will allow you to effectively choose the proper type for your needs.

Three Key Elements of Meeting Agendas

- Basic information like the location, names of expected participants, date, start time and end time of the meeting.
- The topic and the person responsible for it.
- An objective for each item, or for the meeting in general.

Contents of a Meeting Agenda

- Be short, simple, and clear.
- Be informative and practical.
- Have the date, time and location of the meeting.
- State which issues will be discussed and in what order.
- Be the outline for the meeting minutes.

- Help you predict the results of the meeting.

RESOLUTIONS:

A resolution is the final form of a decision taken at a meeting by voting on a motion, with or without amendment. A Resolution must not be confused with a motion. A motion is considered at a meeting, a resolution is the outcome of the discussion. A resolution is binding on the organization. It becomes effective when it is passed but minutes make the evidence of such resolution. Sometimes there is a legal formality, as we find in the Companies Act, to file a copy of a resolution with some appropriate authority (e.g., the Registrar of Companies) to make it effective.

Rules Regarding Resolution-

Every association has to function guided by the resolutions adopted at the meetings at different levels- resolutions passed at general meetings, at executive meetings and at committee meetings, if any. In an Assembly or in Parliament proposed Bills are passed in the forms of resolutions which become the Acts subsequently. Therefore, the importance of resolutions is immense. Certain rules have to be strictly observed for passing resolutions.

1. The drafting of a resolution has to be carried out with great care so that the purpose or meaning of the resolution is easily and clearly understandable and there is no ambiguity (double meaning). The secretary, who is supposed to be an expert in the line, helps in the drafting process. The motion itself shall be drafted in such a manner that it can be adopted as a perfect resolution. This is particularly true for a formal resolution.
2. There are different styles and forms of drafting a resolution. Any one style can be followed. It is desirable that a formal resolution is drafted in a specialized style.
3. A resolution must be entered in the Minute Book in verbatim, i.e., word for word.
4. Once a resolution is passed it cannot be revoked or cancelled either at the same meeting or at any subsequent meeting by passing another resolution.

Types of Resolutions-

Broadly speaking, resolutions are of two types:

1. **Ordinary Resolution:**

   This type of resolution has the following characteristics:

   a. This can be passed by a simple majority of votes and even by a margin of one vote. It can be passed (or lost) by the casting vote of the chairman.
   b. This type of resolution is necessary to take decisions on ordinary matters of the association
   c. This is the most common type of resolution.
   d. Formalities for passing such a resolution (unlike a special resolution) are not so strict.

2. **Special Resolution:**

   This type of resolution has the following characteristics:

   a. It needs a specific margin of votes to be passed. For example- two-third majority or three- fourth majority. Every association in its bye-laws mentions what shall be the margin. There may be statutory rules too. For example, the Companies Act states that there shall be three- fourths majority out of the members present (in person or by proxy) and voting. According to our Constitution, any Article of the Constitution can be altered by two-thirds majority of all the members of Parliament.
   b. Such resolutions are necessary when any decision has to be taken affecting the very constitution of the organization, e.g., altering the objects of the organization.
   c. This type of resolution is not commonly necessary.
   d. There may be strict formalities to be followed for the purpose (as found in the Companies Act).

Concept of types of resolutions comes mostly from the Companies Act. There are various types of resolutions mentioned in the Companies Act, mainly applicable to members' meetings.

Resolutions as found in the Companies Act:

1. Ordinary Resolution:

According to Sec. 189(1), an ordinary resolution is that which can be passed at a general meeting by simple majority (including a casting vote of the chairman, if any), votes being cast by the members present either in person or by proxy and either by show of hands or by poll.

2. Special Resolution:

According to Sec. 189(2), a special resolution is that which can be passed at a general meeting, votes being cast by the members present either in person or by proxy and either by show of hands or by poll, provided that (a) in the agenda it is mentioned that the resolution shall be passed as a special resolution, (b) a notice has been duly issued and (c) three-fourth of the votes cast are in favour of the resolution.

It has to be noted that at a Board meeting there is no question of any special resolution. But, sometimes to pass a particular type of resolution the consent of all the directors present is necessary. (In the past, special resolution was known as extraordinary resolution).

3. Resolution with Special Notice:

According to the Companies Act, certain resolutions require a special notice for their validity. The resolution itself may be passed as an ordinary resolution. The notice for a members meeting is prepared and issued by the Board of Directors (the secretary does it in practice) and the agenda is included in the notice.

If any member who wants to move any motion at the meeting must be given the opportunity to do it and generally for that this Section has been provided. According to Sec. 190, certain resolutions, as wanted by the Act or as mentioned in the articles, require special notice.

It means that a member, intending to move a resolution, shall give a notice to the company at least fourteen days before the meeting and the company shall circulate the notice of the resolution to all the members at least seven days before the meeting.

Suppose, a director is to retire by rotation and his name has been mentioned in the notice as offering for re-election A member wants to propose the name of another person. He must send the name of that person at least fourteen days before the meeting and the company shall circulate the name at least seven days before the meeting (Sec. 257).

4. Resolution by Circulation:

The Board of Directors of a Company (or the members of a committee appointed out of the directors of a company) may pass a resolution without holding a meeting. This can be done by circulating a draft of the resolution together with necessary papers, if any, to all the directors (or the members of the committee) at their usual address in India, and who are in India.

MINUTES:

Minutes, also known as minutes of meeting (abbreviation MoM), protocols or, informally, notes, are the instant written record of a meeting or hearing. They typically describe the events of the meeting and may include a list of attendees, a statement of the issues considered by the participants, and related responses or decisions for the issues.

The name "minutes" possibly derives from the Latin phrase minuta scriptura (literally "small writing") meaning "rough notes". Minutes may be created during the meeting by a typist or court reporter, which may use shorthand notation and then prepare the minutes and issue them to the participants afterwards. Alternatively, the meeting can be audio recorded, video recorded, or a group's appointed or informally assigned secretary may take notes, with minutes prepared later. Many government agencies use minutes recording software to record and prepare all minutes in real-time.

POINTS TO REMEMBER:

Requisites of a Meeting-

If the business transacted at a meeting is to be valid and legally binding, the meeting itself must be validly held. A meeting will be considered to be validly held, if:

- It is properly convened by proper authority.
- Proper notice must be served.
- Proper quorum must be present in the meeting.
- Proper chairman must preside the meeting.
- Business must be validly transacted at the meeting.
- Proper minutes of the meeting must be prepared.

GLOSSARY:

- **Agenda-** The plan for a meeting, lists the items to be discussed in the order in which they will be discussed.
- **Amendment-** Proposed modification to a motion which is not in conflict with the general thrust of that motion. If the amendment is adopted it becomes part of the original motion (now called 'motion as amended' or 'substantive motion').
- **Apologies-** Formal notifications of inability to attend a meeting.
- **Brainstorming-** A technique used to gather ideas from a group; it involves the members of the group thinking of as many ideas as they can in a short period of time.
- **Business Arising-** Discussion on any matter recorded in the minutes of the previous meeting.
- **Chair-** The person who controls the conduct of the meeting, a sort of umpire.
- **Consensus-** A type of group decision making. It involves coming to a decision acceptable to all members of the group without a vote being taken.
- **Constitution-** A document setting out the fundamental principles governing the running of an organization. It normally includes such things as the goals of the organization, membership requirements, rights and fees, meeting times, voting rights and standing orders for

meetings.

- **General Business**- The body of the meeting where the main objectives of the meeting are discussed.

- **Minutes**- The formal written record of a meeting. Copies are circulated to attendees and those who apologized (and sometimes to other interested parties), and formally confirmed at the next meeting as being a true record.
- **Motion**- A formal statement, usually involving some proposed action, put to a meeting for discussion and subsequent decision by vote.
- **Mover**- The proposer of a motion.
- **Motion of Dissent**- A formal statement involving some proposed action, put to a meeting for discussion and subsequent decision by vote.
- **Other Business**- An item on the agenda (usually the last) that provides an opportunity for those present to suggest additional matters for discussion.
- **Point of Order**- A formal complaint (to the chair person) at a meeting that a speaker is being irrelevant, unduly repetitive, exceeding prescribed time, speaking out of turn or in some way violating standing orders.
- **Procedural motion**- A motion aimed at changing the sequence or timing of events at a meeting, rather than one which addresses an agenda item.
- **Quorum**- Minimum number (or percentage of those invited) required being at a meeting for it to proceed legitimately.

CHAPTER TWELVE

MANAGEMENT INFORMATION SYSTEMS (MIS)

INTRODUCTION:

A management information system (MIS) is a broadly used and applied term for a three-resource system required for effective organization management. The resources are people, information and technology, from inside and outside an organization, with top priority given to people. The system is a collection of information management methods involving computer automation (software and hardware) or otherwise supporting and improving the quality and efficiency of business operations and human decision making. As an area of study, MIS is sometimes referred to as information technology management (IT management) or information services (IS). Neither should be confused with computer science.

WHY MIS?

Managers make decisions and decision-making generally takes a four-fold path-

- Understanding the need for decision or the opportunity.
- Preparing the alternative course of actions.
- Evaluating all the alternative course of actions.

- Deciding the right path for implementation.

MIS is an information system that provides information in the form of standardized reports and displays for the managers. MIS is a broad class of information systems designed to provide information needed for effective decision making. Data and information created from an accounting information system and the reports generated thereon are used to provide accurate, timely and relevant information needed for effective decision making by managers. Management information systems provide information to support management decision making, with the following goals-

- Pre-specified and pre-planned reporting to managers.
- Interactive and ad-hoc support for decision making.
- Critical information for top management.
- MIS is of vital importance to any organization, because –

It emphasizes on the management decision making, not only processing of data generated by business operations.

It emphasizes on the systems framework that should be used for organizing information systems applications.

The purpose of using MIS-

- "A formal method of collecting timely information in a presentable form in order to facilitate effective decision making and implementation, in order to carryout organizational operations for the purpose of achieving the organizational goals". Walter

Kennevan defines MIS as "An MIS is a system designed to provide selected decision- oriented information needed by management to plan, control and evaluate the activities of the corporation. It is designed within a framework that emphasizes profit planning, performance planning and control at all levels."

- MIS is very useful for efficient and effective planning and control functions of the management. Management is the art of getting things done through others. MIS will be instrumental in getting the things done by providing quick and timely information to the management.

- Reports give an idea about the performance of men, materials, machinery, money and management. Reports throw light on the utilization of resources employed in the organization.
- MIS is helpful in controlling costs by giving information about idle time, labor turnover, wastages and losses and surplus capacity.
- By making comparison of actual performance with the standard and budgeted performance, variances are brought to the notice of the management by MIS which can be corrected by taking remedial steps.
- MIS brings to the notice of the management strength (i.e., strong points) of the organization, to take advantage of the opportunities available.
- MIS reports on production statistics regarding rejection, defective and spoilage and their effect on costs and quality of the products.

INFORMATION AS A STRATEGIC RESOURCE:

It is impossible to neglect the impact of information and information technologies on the strategy of companies nowadays because of its important role in competition. Since competitiveness is getting stronger and stronger in most of the industries, new competitors are emerging, the environment is also changing and the expectations of clients are continuously altering, managers are those who should not allow themselves to stay indifferent in such situations.

Today, information can no longer be treated as a source of competitive advantage, but a competitive necessity. It penetrates in all aspects of an organization, crosses data processing and information systems department. The information potential can be realized by the means of appropriate management and knowledge of the organizational and cultural aspects. No automatic profits come from investments in information technologies since management has the responsibility for exploitation of the information technology potential. During the last two decades, companies have learned how to manage financial, human and material resources. The changes of the management of these resources depend on the access, processing and means of information. A receipt of information resource management is impossible to be given, neither is desirable because the approach should be structured and flexible and managers are those who should possess it.

The managers of an organization should be well-informed of the profits of the appropriate information and information technology. The most important questions for them are: What information is needed so that the company can fulfill the set strategic aims? Which skills or products will be an advantage over competitors? What is the current strategy in order to beat competitors? And what information is needed to form it? Successful organizations are those who are learning and adapting and have a flat simple structure and information is inseparable part of their activity. That is why managers should be trained how to use it effectively. Information Resource Management (IRM) defines the way in which the organization will accomplish its business when using different information resources in order to make its short- term strategies. This management is unique even for companies with identical products and/ or services. Information Resource Management includes the management of all kinds of data, numbers, texts, images and sounds available in making the proper strategy at a certain moment. This is why managers are responsible for the provisions of the appropriate information concerning the business and decision making.

Information impacts on all aspects of the organization: marketing, distribution, production, operations management, management economics, finance, public policy, industry dynamics, office automation, human resource management as shown on the figure above. The wheel is spinning round and in its centre is Information Resource Management. Information and communication technologies provide continuous information flow, which the organization should use in forming its corporate strategy and accomplishing its management activities in decision making. Of great importance for organizations is their flexible management style.

That is why a great quantity of information and its optimal use is needed especially by decision-makers in the processes of decision making. The more information is used the better for the company. The better the instrument of using this information, the better the decision will be. The better the decision will be the less the risks for the company are. For this reason, information is an important resource which should be managed appropriately and thus it increases the company's chances of success. The effective management is day to day even every minute because the environment is changing very fast and it should respond to its quick changes. Consequently, short run strategies are needed because of this and long run plans are no longer made. In this sense, the planning of information resources is of great value and should satisfy the needs of the organization.

Most of the strategies aim to increase production, to increase sales or to increase profit and these can be achieved by current use of information. For example, a number of the applications of information technologies lead to a great decrease in costs since mediators are eliminated. So distribution costs no longer exist, personnel costs are diminished exclusively and also the deadlines of delivery are lessened to a great extent. Consequently, the prices of the products/ services are decreased substantially which means that people are encouraged to buy more. This eventually increases sales and profit of the company and of course the quantity of production needed should be greater. When production is higher the costs per product or service is less and the profit is higher. The assimilation of information is a challenge for every manager because the participation of information in company management leads to a higher effectiveness and better results in forming the competitive strategy. Managers should pay attention to six basic problems concerning information and its use in organization:

- Information impacts different companies in different ways. This is the reason why management approaches and instruments and their use should be chosen appropriately.
- Coordination and control of information should be established.
- Education of the organization in using information in forming short run strategies.
- Decisions about building or buying of appropriate information technologies should be precisely made and information about them should be collected.

USE OF INFORMATION FOR COMPETITIVE ADVANTAGE:

A company gains competitive advantage by providing a product or service in a way that customers gain more value than with a competitor. However, it is not information technology that gives a company a competitive advantage; it's the way they use information technology that makes the difference. Businesses need to use information technology innovatively.

Innovation is the process of devising ways to do things in new and creative ways. Using information technology to tackle a business problem the same way the other companies have been doing is probably not going to give a firm the competitive advantage. The company has to invent or develop creative ways to create something new their competitors don't have yet. Below listed points represents the use of Information Technology (IT) in Competitive Advantage as-

1. The CEO's Attitude toward Information Technology-

The CEO's vision can influence how managers think about things within their company, including information technology. If the CEO understands that IT can be a powerful competitive weapon, a message is relayed to the entire organization; that coming up with creative IT ideas can lead to a company's growth and improved customer satisfaction. Company leadership is very important in determining its competitive advantage using information technology.

2.To bridge the gap between business people and technical people-

Business people must understand the use of Information technology to gain competitive advantage. In this case, they work hand in hand with a technical team to achieve this goal. Designing an information system that gives the competitive advantage needs at least two things. First, it requires an understanding of the business problem you are trying to solve. Second, it requires knowledge of available technologies to use in designing a creative solution for the business problem. It's beneficial for business people to study management information systems (MIS). Doing so will help them better analyse technical issues if the need arises.

3. To view business problems from another Perspective-

It is imperative to view a business problem from the perspective of your customers. These are the owners of your business, not you, because, without them, the business will not survive. IT can provide businesses with valuable information to better understand the needs and requirements of their customers and stakeholders. Being informed of limitations and inconveniences experienced by the customer should result in the more effective use of resources to resolve these issues.

4. **Use in Creative Designing-**

Creative design of an IT system is one that solves the business problem in a new and highly effective way. One of the biggest mistakes most business people make when designing new information systems is to come up with a design that is typical, something very similar to what other companies are doing.

INFORMATION MANAGEMENT:

Information management (IM) is the process of collecting, storing, managing and maintaining information in all its forms. Information Management is a broad term that incorporates policies and procedures for centrally managing and sharing information among different individuals, organizations and/or information systems throughout the information life cycle. Information management may also be called information asset management.

Information management is generally an enterprise information system concept, where an organization produces, owns and manages a suite of information. The information can be in the form of physical data (such as papers, documents and books), or digital data assets. Information management deals with the level and control of an organization's governance over its information assets. Information management is typically achieved through purpose-built information management systems and by supporting business processes and guidelines. Moreover, IM also focuses on how that information is shared and delivered to various recipients, including individuals and different computing devices such as an organization's website, computers, servers, applications and/or mobile devices.

As per the definition given by Davis in 1997, Information Management (IM) is the process by which relevant information is provided to decision-makers in a timely manner. Information management has largely been defined from an information systems perspective and equated with the management of information technology. IM is a generic term that encompasses all the systems and processes within organizations for the creation and use of corporate information.

DECISION-MAKING:

Decision-making is a cognitive process that results in the selection of a course of action among several alternative scenarios. Decision-making is a daily activity for any human being. There is no exception about that. When it comes to business organizations, decision-making is a habit and a process as well. Effective and successful decisions result in profits, while unsuccessful ones cause losses. Therefore, corporate decision-making is the most critical process in any organization.

In a decision-making process, we choose one course of action from a few possible alternatives. In the process of decision-making, we may use many tools, techniques, and perceptions. In addition, we may make our own private decisions or may prefer a collectivedecision. Usually, decision-making is hard. Majority of corporate decisions involve some level of dissatisfaction or conflict with another party. Let's have a look at the decision-making process in detail. Following are the important steps of the decision-making process. Each step may be supported by different tools and techniques.

Step 1 – Identification of the Purpose of the Decision
In this step, the problem is thoroughly analyzed. There are a couple of questions one should ask when it comes to identifying the purpose of the decision.

What exactly is the problem?

Why the problem should be solved?

Who are the affected parties of the problem?

Does the problem have a deadline or a specific time-line?

Step 2 – Information Gathering
A problem of an organization will have many stakeholders. In addition, there can be dozens of factors involved and affected by the problem.

In the process of solving the problem, you will have to gather as much as information related to the factors and stakeholders involved in the problem. For the process of information gathering, tools such as 'Check Sheets' can be effectively used.

Step 3 – Principles for Judging the Alternatives
In this step, the baseline criteria for judging the alternatives should be set up. When it comes to defining the criteria, organizational goals as well as the corporate culture should be taken into consideration.

As an example, profit is one of the main concerns in every decision-making process. Companies usually do not make decisions that reduce profits, unless it is an exceptional case. Likewise, baseline principles should be identified related to the problem in hand.

Step 4 – Brainstorm and Analyze the Choices

For this step, brainstorming to list down all the ideas is the best option. Before the idea generation step, it is vital to understand the causes of the problem and prioritization of causes.

For this, you can make use of Cause-and-Effect diagrams and Pareto Chart tool. Cause-and- Effect diagram helps you to identify all possible causes of the problem and Pareto chart helps you to prioritize and identify the causes with the highest effect.

Then, you can move on generating all possible solutions (alternatives) for the problem in hand.

Step 5 – Evaluation of Alternatives

Use your judgment principles and decision-making criteria to evaluate each alternative. In this step, experience and effectiveness of the judgment principles come into play. You need to compare each alternative for their positives and negatives.

Step 6 – Select the Best Alternative

Once you go through from Step 1 to Step 5, this step is easy. In addition, the selection of the best alternative is an informed decision since you have already followed a methodology to derive and select the best alternative.

Step 7 – Execute the decision

Convert your decision into a plan or a sequence of activities. Execute your plan by yourself or with the help of subordinates.

Step 8 – Evaluate the Results

Evaluate the outcome of your decision. See whether there is anything you should learn and then correct in future decision making. This is one of the best practices that will improve your decision-making skills.

MODELS OF DECISION MAKING:

The decision-making process though a logical one is a difficult task. All decisions can be categorized into the following three basic models.

- The Rational/Classical Model.
- The Administrative or Bounded Rationality Model.

- Herbert Simon's Model.

All models are beneficial for understanding the nature of decision-making processes in enterprises or organizations. All models are based on certain assumptions on which the decisions are taken.

1. The Rational/Classical Model

The rational model is the first attempt to know the decision-making-process. It is considered by some as the classical approach to understand the decision-making process. The classical model gave various steps in decision-making process which have been discussed earlier. Features of Classical Model-

- Problems are clear.
- Objectives are clear.
- People agree on criteria and weights.
- All alternatives are known.
- All consequences can be anticipated.
- Decision makes are rational.

2. The Administrative or Bounded Rationality Model

Decision-making involve the achievement of a goal. Rationality demands that the decision- maker should properly understand the alternative courses of action for reaching the goals. He should also have full information and the ability to analyze properly various alternative courses of action in the light of goals sought. There should also be a desire to select the best solutions by selecting the alternative which will satisfy the goal achievement.

Herbert A. Simon defines rationality in terms of objective and intelligent action. It is characterized by behavioral nexus between ends and means. If appropriate means are chosen to reach desired ends the decision is rational.

Bounded Rationality model is based on the concept developed by Herbert Simon. This model does not assume individual rationality in the decision process. Instead, it assumes that people, while they may seek the best solution, normally settle for much less, because the decisions they confront typically demand greater information, time, processing capabilities than they possess. They settle for "bounded rationality or limited rationality in decisions. This model is based on certain basic concepts.

Sequential Attention to alternative solution: Normally it is the tendency for people to examine possible solution one at a time instead of identifying all possible solutions and stop searching once an acceptable (though not necessarily the best) solution is found.

Heuristic: These are the assumptions that guide the search for alternatives into areas that have a high probability for yielding success.

Satisficing: Herbert Simon called this "satisficing" that is picking a course of action that is satisfactory or "good enough" under the circumstances. It is the tendency for decision makers to accept the first alternative that meets their minimally acceptable requirements rather than pushing them further for an alternative that produces the best results. Satisficing is preferred for decisions of small significance when time is the major constraint or where most of the alternatives are essentially similar. Thus, while the rational or classic model indicates how decisions should be made (i.e. it works as a prescriptive model), it falls somewhat short concerning how decisions are actually made (i.e. as a descriptive model).

3. Herbert Simon's Model

This model is linked with the decision-making process which explains the core of the decision making and used as the base for explaining the decision-making process. According, the Herbert Simon Model, the process of the decision making consists of the following phases –

i. **The Intelligence Phase-** In this phase, the various activities for finding out the problems related to the searching of the operating environment is involved. By this, the identification of the various conditions can be done which ultimately helps in taking the decisions at the different levels. Extensive and the comprehensive database is must for the intelligence phase, making this phase very suitable for searching or scanning of the environment.

In this phase, the type of the environment forms a very major factor and hence the types of the environment can be categorized as the follows-

a. The Societal Environment: Mainly includes the economic, the legal and the social environment and it is this type of the environment in which the organization operates.

b. The Competitive Environment: Includes the understanding and the analyzing of the characteristics, the trends and the behavior of or at the market place and also the various players of the market in which the organization operates.

c. The Organizational Environment: Includes the various capabilities, the strengths, the weaknesses, the constraints and the various other factors that affect the ability of the organization to discharge or operate its various types of the activities.

ii. **The Design Phase**- The inventing, developing and analysing of the various alternatives or the solutions to the particular problem forms a major part of this phase. Various steps to be followed in this phase can be summarized as the follows-

a. Support in getting the in-depth knowledge of the problem.

b. A correct model of the situation can be made and the assumptions of the model need to be tested.

c. Support for the generation of the solutions can be obtained by-manipulation of the model for the development of the insights and creation of the database retrieval system.

iii. **The Choice Phase**- The selection of a specific alternative or the course of the action from the ones which have been generated and considered during the design phase, takes place during this phase. The choice procedure and the implementation of the chosen alternative form a very major part of the choice phase. The flow of the activities takes place from the intelligence phase to the design phase and then finally to the choice phase. But, one very important point that must be remembered here is that at any phase there may be a return to a previous phase.

POINTS TO REMEMBER:

- MIS is an information system that provides information in the form of standardized reports and displays for the managers.

- MIS is very useful for efficient and effective planning and control functions of the management.
- MIS is sometimes referred to as information technology management (IT management) or information services (IS).
- Data and information created from an accounting information system and the reports generated thereon are used to provide accurate, timely and relevant information needed for effective decision making by managers.
- Business people must understand the use of Information technology to gain competitive advantage.
- Information management is generally an enterprise information system concept, where an organization produces, owns and manages a suite of information.
- Information management is a generic term that encompasses all the systems and processes within organizations for the creation and use of corporate information.
- Information management has largely been defined from an information systems perspective and equated with the management of information technology.
- Decision-making is a cognitive process that results in the selection of a course of action among several alternative scenarios.
- In a decision-making process, we choose one course of action from a few possible alternatives.

GLOSSARY:

- Management Information System- MIS is an information system that provides information in the form of standardized reports and displays for the managers. MIS is a broad class of information systems designed to provide information needed for effective decision making.
- Purpose of MIS - MIS is very useful for efficient and effective planning and control functions of the management. Management is the art of getting things done through others. MIS will be instrumental in getting the things done by providing quick and timely information to the management.

- Use of Information - A company gains competitive advantage by providing a product or service in a way that customers gain more value than with a competitor. However, it is not information technology that gives a company a competitive advantage; it's the way they use information technology that makes the difference. Businesses need to use information technology innovatively.
- Information Management - Information management is typically achieved through Purpose-built information management systems and by supporting business processes and guidelines.
- Decision-Making - Decision-making is a daily activity for any human being. There is no exception about that. When it comes to business organizations, decision-making is a habit and a process as well. Effective and successful decisions result in profits, while unsuccessful ones cause losses. Therefore, corporate decision-making is the most critical process in any organization.
- Decision-Making Models - The decision-making process though a logical one is a difficult task. All decisions can be categorized into the following three basic models. Rational/Classical model, administrative or bounded rationality model and Herbert Simon's Models.

About The Author: Dr Anshumali Pandey

Dr Anshumali Pandey, PHD, Author.

Dr. Anshumali Pandey, is a renowned & reliable name in the field of Education, Hospitality, Tourism and Tribal Food. He is a Teacher and Chef by profession, and also an Author, a Business Auditor, and an avid culinary traveller to the Indian Sub continental hinterlands. Dr. Anshumali Pandey is a Hospitality Educator (PhD) who specialises in Higher Education, Office Administration, Pay roll, HR, Labour Laws, Audit, and Procurement & Tender Process. He is an Author with 44 Publications consisting of 29 Books.

The books written by Dr Anshumali Pandey are essentially a banquet arising from an experience of over 25 years of Professional life and have boiled down to crisp and accurate writing on his favourite subjects. Hospitality Sector champion requires to be a specialist in many fields and Dr Pandey is one of them. His knowledge is evident from the spectrum of subjects which he has chosen for his books so far, which ranges from being a specialist chef, to Master of Human resources, to Education and to love for

children, and topped with Spirituality.
Books written by the Author are –

1. Theory of Indian Cookery
2. Beauty and Irony of Silvassa Tourism
3. A Short Indian Food Story
4. Be Your Own Guide to Indian Cuisine
5. Cookery Fundamentals
6. History of Indian Food
7. The Great Indian Story Book for Children
8. Personal Budget: Easy Work Book
9. Online Classes Log Book
10. Dictionary Making Work Book for School Children
11. The Lazy Bed
12. Hindu Dharm (हिन्दू धर्म) (In Hindi Language)
13. Where is my coffee?
14. Your First Job is Never your Last (Volume 1)
15. You are Almost There (Quick Fix Resume and Interview Hacks)
16. Working for the Enemy? - A lesson in Career Management
17. Public Speaking for the Young
18. A Date With Coffee
19. How to be The Best Hotel Front Office Employee
20. Diploma in Food Production, The complete Syllabus
21. Diploma in F&B Service, The Complete Syllabus
22. Diploma in Front Office, The Complete Syllabus
23. The Time to Speak is Now
24. Munshi Premchand (Short Stories in English)
25. The Housekeeping Department, Text Book
26. Hitchhiker's Guide to Trekking in Uttarakhand
27. Uttarakhand, A divine Land for a Reason
28. Bachhon ke liye rochak kahaniyan (बच्चों के लिए रोचक कहानियाँ) (In Hindi Language)
29. Basic Communication Skills of English
30. The Basic Office Organisation Book for Start-ups

Connect with me: anshumali.pandey@gmail.com
https://notionpress.com/author/337004

Please scan this QR Code to check updated information.

About The Author: Shambhu Nath Gautam

Mr. Shambhu Nath Gautam, Author.

Shambhu Nath Gautam: Principal, Food Craft Institute Khajuraho, Under Ministry of Tourism, Govt. of M.P & Govt. of India.

Education: DHM, MBA (Hotel Management), PG Dip in Hotel Management, PG Dip in HRM (Gold Medallist), MA English Litt.

About: The author is an alumni on IHM Lucknow and Pusa with vast academic experience. The journey started with doing Hotel Management from IHM Lucknow 1994-95 and then IHM Pusa 1996-1997. After completing Graduation he worked in Mehmaan Restaurant as Assistant Restaurant Manager for more than 1 year, after that joined Food Craft Institute Ajmer as Assistant Lecturer and Lecturer from 1998 till 2018. He was also having additional charge as OSD/Member Secretary of State Institute of Hotel Management, Sawai Madhopur from March 2014 till March 2018. At present author is working as Principal of Food Craft Institute Khajuraho, from April 2018.

The author has trained, mentored and guided more than 2500 students in which many of them have achieved success in Hotel Industry and are working as Top hospitality professionals and are settled in India as well as abroad. The author's core area of teaching is Food Production and Bakery. Shambhu Nath Gautam is well known in Hotel Industry as an industry expert in his subject.